From the Library of Roderick A. Hawkins

The Islands of the Sulu Sea

by
Kurt Rose

THE GLENCANNON PRESS

Copyright © 1993 by Kurt Rose
Published by The Glencannon Press
P.O. Box 341, Palo Alto, CA 94302

10 9 8 7 6 5 4 3 2 1

Library of Congress Catalog Card Number 93-61096

ISBN   0-9637586-1-6

The front and back cover photos were provided by the Department of Tourism of the Philippines. Illustrations by Sherry Hecht.

All rights reserved. Printed in the United States of America. No part of this book may be used or reproduced, stored in a retrieval system, or transmitted in any form or by any means, electronic, mechanical, photocopying, recording or otherwise in any manner whatsoever without written permission except in the case of brief quotations embodied in critical articles or reviews.

Dedication

To the dreams of youth.

Kurt Rose aboard the Gospel Ship in the 1930's. From the author's collection.

"I have seen the sunset, stained with mystic wonders,
Illumine the rolling waves with long purple forms,
I have seen starry archipelagoes! and islands
Whose Heavens are opened to the voyager."

Arthur Rimbaud

Table of Contents

The Call of the Sea 1
Stowaways 8
Suez 14
The Indian Ocean 21
World Map 28
Manila, the First Time 30
Shanghai 35
Alone In Vladivostok 42
Hitchhiking In Asia 45
A Year In Manila 56
The Gospel Ship 59
Palawan 66
Crocodile Sound 72
Tropical Medicine 79
Lost in the Jungle 86
Map of the Philippines 97
Borneo 98
Sulu 109
Zamboanga 116
Return to Manila 124
The Leper Colony 130
Aground 140
The Moro Princess 146
A Moro Dance 155
The Sea Gypsies 163
The Hadjii 168
Return to Shanghai 174
I Become Engaged 179
Rites and Rituals 184
The Engine Explodes 190
The Ship Sinks 195
The Voyage Ends 203
About The Ship 205
About The Author 208
Glossary 209
Index 212

The Islands of the Sulu Sea

1

The Call of the Sea

Day was breaking as I squirmed into my heavy, tight overcoat, smiled at my sister Gretel, and opened the apartment door on my way to the far countries. Halfway down the stairs I looked back and saw her following me. At the front door I stopped and said farewell once more. Abruptly, as I turned the knob, a vague yet disturbing sadness came over me. I looked at my sister. She stood quietly, her eyes large in the semi-darkness of the ill-lighted hall. We gazed at each other gravely, wordlessly. On an impulse, for the only time in my life, I placed my arm around her shoulders, kissed her on the cheek, and murmured, "I love you very much." Then, embarrassed, I stepped hastily into the dismal February dawn.

It was the winter of 1931. I was seventeen years old.

The streets glistened with wetness. Fanned by a light north wind, fog swirled around me in ragged wisps, its dank cold penetrating my thick clothing. My heart was heavy.

My sister Gretel. This was taken about the time I left Hamburg. She was fourteen. From the author's collection.

Walking quickly, I soon reached the fog-shrouded harbor. The ship which I had signed on as engine boy for a voyage to the Orient lay somewhere in midstream, invisible in the gray-white vapor.

As I stood shivering at the ferry wharf another thickly-clad seaman joined me. Presently a dozen more rough, silent men were shuffling about the small jetty, smoking, chewing, coughing, staring into the black, ice-pocked water.

Wondering which of these men might be my shipmates, I was about to strike up a conversation when the ferry poked her square snout through the fog blanket. Quickly tying up, she disembarked a horde of sailors who had arrived during the night. They were distinctly different from those about to leave. Happy and noisy, they carried large and small objects wrapped in gunny sacks, bamboo matting, newspapers with strange characters, or brightly-dyed cloth. A small monkey, the picture of abject fear and misery, huddled against the fur collar of a white-haired, ruddy-faced man.

Then they were gone, their gay chatter and curses echoing ever fainter from the sheds, as we filed aboard the small ferry, each man singing out the name of his ship: "*Cardiff, Kobenhavn, Nordwind, Tricolor, Lidvaard.*" The voices were gravelly and often little more than a croak. I wondered how the ferryboat skipper, leaning from the wheelhouse window, could understand them. Anxious to be one of the hardy seamen I tried growling the name of my ship, but my still-high voice refused to cooperate. It cracked in a most embarrassing manner as I squared my shoulders and called out, "*Eta Rickmers.*"

After waiting a good half hour for additional passengers who didn't come, the ferry backed into the stream, turned and headed into the fog. Her destination was the row of buoys in the center of one of the many arms of the big harbor of Hamburg. Presently a green, blunt-nosed steamer hove into sight, the name *Eta Rickmers* in big, white, rust-spotted letters on the bow. I picked up my suitcase and looked around. None of my fellow passengers made a move to disembark. The ferry scraped along the steamer's riveted plates, knocking off rust blisters, nudged the gangway sharply, then backed off almost instantly. I had perhaps five seconds to fling my suitcase and myself onto the platform. Turning, I saw the boat was already yards away and coming about, white water seething under her squat stern.

Climbing to the top of the gangway, I looked along the decks. The ship was a "three-islander." That is, she had a raised forecastle, a midships house and a raised poop deck. Between these three islands were the cargo hatches. Half a dozen seamen were already at work on the fore deck, clearing away splintered dunnage, frayed bits of rope and empty milk tins.

The drab, littered deck was not an inspiring sight. Neither was the huge pile of coal heaped on the bunker hatches, a mound of glistening blackness which looked sinister and somehow foreboding. Passing the bunkers, I smelled a most heavenly aroma and saw at the same instant, the one place a teenager holds dearest, the kitchen -- or, in this case, the galley. I stopped, entranced as only a hungry seventeen-year-old can be. Then I remembered I hadn't eaten breakfast. The cook and his boy were chattering most pleasantly. The sizzle and sputter of eggs frying and the soft scraping of spatula against pan were extraordinarily sweet sounds, as I stood there clutching my suitcase.

Reluctantly I continued aft, past a row of portholes behind which I guessed lay the cabins of the ship's officers. Then down the after well deck, up the ladder to the poop deck, and down the narrow companionway to the crew's quarters. The alleyway at the bottom was lighted by a single electric bulb. The doors on each side were closed. I stood, unsure of which one to open, until my eyes fell on a chipped, enamelled sign over the port door. "FIREMEN AND TRIMMERS," it proclaimed. I looked at the other sign. It said, "SEAMEN." The right door was relatively clean. The left door bore the imprint of black hands and fingers. Nervously licking my lips, I opened the left door.

The room was large, but low and dingy. The bulkheads were lined with lockers and double-tiered bunks. A long wooden table, scrubbed to a light yellow, flanked by two unpainted benches, stood in the center of the room directly beneath a closed skylight. On the port bulkhead were three small, dirty portholes, also closed. A long, narrow, foot-high box bisected the room. I later learned this was the rudder chain casing.

The murmur of conversation stopped when I entered but resumed almost immediately. A few men were sitting at the table, fingers curled around steaming coffee cups. One tough looking oldster stood up and pointed to an upper bunk.

"Yours," was all he said.

The Islands of the Sulu Sea

Then he gestured to a side door. "The pans are in there. Get the breakfast."

The small side room had a concrete floor with a drainhole in the center. There was a rough shelf under the porthole and another wider one along the bulkhead separating the pantry, if one could call it by so grand a name, from the living quarters. Overhead, on a board bolted to the bare plates, were a number of hooks for the coffee mugs and anything else with a handle. Having examined the dreary cubicle, I took a somewhat tremulous breath, picked up the three nested pans and headed for the galley. Thus began my first day aboard a tramp steamer on the Far East run.

The quarters, which would be my home for several months, measured thirty feet in length and half that wide. In it, sixteen men -- nine firemen, six coaltrimmers, and one boy (me) -- ate, slept, played and sometimes argued. I soon learned that hardship was the rule, not the exception. Salt pork was the main course four times a week. There was no running water in the single wash room except for a salt water tap. Each of the six tubs bolted to the bulkheads had a cold water pump.

It was my duty, near the end of the day watches, to fill two buckets with cold water from the galley pump and heat it by immersing a steam pipe in the bucket and turning on the steam. Then, in good weather and foul, under blazing tropical sun or in raging snowstorms, I toted the buckets aft for the "black gang's" bath. This was in addition to the water I had to bring for washing the dishes and general cleanup.

In short order I learned the rest of my duties. Peel a bucket of potatoes every day, and the peels had better be thin. Otherwise the cook would boil them in their skins and I would hear about it. Wash sixteen plates, cups, forks, spoons, knives, four pans, ladles and other utensils three times each day, and half as many between meals. Keep the white paint on the doors and bulkheads white, an almost impossible task in the black gang quarters. Clean the latrine, a crude six-seat affair on the poop deck, daily. Haul ashes from the fire room every day at 2 p.m. Keep the portholes of the engineers' cabins bright and do odd jobs for the chief engineer. All for five dollars a month, with twenty percent of that taken out for income tax!

But none of that mattered. I was off on a long voyage to the ends of the earth, and when I returned I would be burdened with the most exotic of presents. When I returned! Now and then, as I did my chores during the morning hours, an inexplicable sadness stole over me. And when we sailed, in mid-afternoon on the twenty-fourth day of February — the anniversary of my mother's death — I watched through tear-filled eyes as the waterfront crept slowly by and wondered at the strange ache in my heart.

An hour later our anchor splashed into the muddy waters of the Elbe. The steamer swung into the current and lay still. Now that Hamburg was no longer in sight, my spirits rose. A short distance away I spotted a two-masted schooner, also at anchor. I smiled, for it reminded me of my first ship, the *Martha W*. It was on her that I acquired my Seaman's Book without which there was no hope of ever sailing on a steamer. I remembered pouring boiling water along the sides of the ship to melt some of the ice that impeded her progress through the freezing North Sea. I also remembered the night I almost wrecked the ship. Running parallel with the coast of Denmark, homesick, seasick, wet and cold, I was given the wheel. It was 8 p.m. and my instructions were to steer for a brilliant star directly ahead. The compass light was too dim to see the card. At eleven thirty the mate appeared, looked about, promptly slapped me, then spun the wheel.

"What are you trying to do, you dog, wreck the ship? Look!" he roared, pointing.

I bit my lip. We were headed directly for the rocky coast. I had steered for the same star the entire watch as it traveled across the heavens.

The following morning two barges approached the steamer and were made fast, one on the port side of number one hatch, the other on the starboard side of number two. From them two hundred tons of dynamite and blasting caps were stowed in the 'tween decks; one hundred tons for Hong Kong, the rest for Yokohama. At 5 p.m. the last of the stevedores dropped into a waiting launch, the barges were cast off, and half an hour later, with three hoarse roars from the whistle, we sailed in the murky dusk toward the North Sea.

2

Stowaways

I slept uneasily while my stomach heaved in unison with the motions of the ship. I was awakened, not overly gently, at six o'clock the next morning. Sitting up, I shuddered. No longer on my back, wave after wave of nausea suddenly poured over me. The air in the room was stagnant and foul. All the openings were shut because of the cold air and heavy seas. Even the single ventilator was closed with a piece of canvas stretched over its neck. Dressing hurriedly, I held my breath, clenched my teeth against the almost unbearable pressure from my stomach and rushed up the stairs and to the rail.

Relieved momentarily of the wrenching within, I wiped the sweat from my forehead, gulped the cold, clean air, and looked around. It was misty, with about a mile of visibility. From the swirling whiteness ahead, green waves came racing toward the ship, their foaming tops blown flat by the gale. I glanced at the bridge where a lone figure was hunched against the wind on the port wing. I later learned that, a bare half hour before, as the first sickly light of dawn struggled from the darkness, that same officer had stood, his face deathly pale, one hand grasping the whistle lanyard, the other laying flat against the window pane, as a huge tanker bored through the fog, directly in the path of our wallowing steamer. Somehow the *Eta's* frantic maneuvers were perfectly duplicated by the tanker. Our whistle signals were lost in the howl of the storm. Collision seemed inevitable. The tanker, executing a last-moment swing to starboard, surged past with mere yards to spare. Afterward the helmsman saw the pallor in the third mate's face by the faint light of the compass. But before breakfast was finished, everyone knew about it. No blame, not one word of censure was laid upon the third mate. He did everything possible and after that could only stop the engines and stare helplessly, mutely contemplating the specter of collision, of twenty thousand tons of oil and steel tearing into four hundred tons of dynamite and caps. But tragedy was averted while most of us slept — at the brink of eternity.

Approaching the English Channel the weather deteriorated visibly. I dreaded the days ahead. Thirty-six hours through the North Sea, I was told, thirty-six through the Channel, another thirty-six across the Bay of Biscay, and thirty-six more to Cape Sao Vicente on the southern tip of Portugal.

"And bad weather all the way," my informant gleefully concluded.

I hoped he would be proved wrong, but he was right. Throughout the length of the Channel, over the wide Biscay Bay, and until we turned eastward to Gibraltar, the sea roared insanely, pawing at the rivets, clawing the rigging, smashing, tearing, hammering flesh and steel alike until existence became a nightmare of foam and water, of soot and steam, of wrenching metal and splintering wood. But through it all, the tired triple-expansion engine never faltered though she groaned and grated and wheezed. The pressure in the old boilers never dropped below seventy-five pounds to the square inch. The clink of sluice bar against grating and the slam of furnace doors never ceased. And in the Bay of Biscay, when a ruptured pipe poured live steam into the engine room, the leak was patched in an hour. Granted, it was an hour in which the sweat ran into the eyes of the laboring engineers and bare flesh sizzled and hissed on contact with hot metal, but the leak was patched.

After three days of unadulterated misery I would have welcomed death with joy. One dreary evening, a black wave-lashed rock came into view. I felt like flinging myself into the wild sea and swimming for that barren ground. Instead, I drew a trembling breath and went down into the foul smelling quarters and the still more odorous pantry. After doing the supper dishes, I tumbled, sweating and sick, into my bunk, and shut my eyes tightly. Although I could no longer see the swaying bunk curtains or the emergency lamps gyrating in their gimbals, I felt every pitch and roll. And, as if to make certain that I would indeed be aware of it all, the propeller beneath my bunk raced as the stern lifted and the blades lost their bite, then abruptly slowed to almost a standstill as the ship settled back. The irregular throbbing of the screw, the scraping of the rudder chain along the deck, the groaning of the working ship, the constant thunder of wave against hull, and the violent churning in my stomach made sleep virtually impossible. When, in the early morning hours, my tortured body at last yielded to fatigue and I dropped into sleep, even then was I conscious of the motion and the din. I was, therefore, overjoyed when, alerted by a shipmate at sundown, I spotted the yellow-white beam of Sao Vicente light at about 8 p.m. Miraculously, with the calming of the sea soon thereafter, my sickness and despondency disappeared. My appetite, which vanished the moment we entered the

The Islands of the Sulu Sea

North Sea a week earlier, found me, bringing with it my spirits which also sank out of sight at about the same time.

Before midnight the steamer swung into a southeasterly course to bring us into the Strait of Gibraltar and the Mediterranean Sea. We were on the new course less than an hour when a huge liner appeared behind us. Even at that distance and despite the darkness of the overcast night we knew the great ship was following in our wake. It became disturbingly apparent that our presence was undetected. A deckhand stepped to the sternlight and, finding it dark, ran toward the bridge. The liner, now appallingly close, came full on, her bow wave gleaming on the black water, her ports and windows ablaze with golden light. She was doing a good twenty knots, twice our own speed — a thirty thousand ton greyhound racing through the night, the distance between us growing smaller and smaller. Abruptly, a hoarse blast shattered the stillness, as the officer on our bridge yanked at the lanyard. A white plume of steam, illuminated by the mastlight billowed from the funnel. The liner held her course. I glanced the length of our ship. Not a light showed except the faint reflection of the running lights from the shrouds. The liner, P&O's *Rawalpindi*, we discovered later, was now so close we could hear the hissing of her bow wave. Her red and green navigation lights glared balefully like the mismatched eyes of some heathen god. We retreated from the taffrail, confident that another two minutes would plunge our ship into disaster. Then our ship blew a series of quick, short whistle blasts, the international danger signal. This alerted the bridge of the great ship, for her bow fell abruptly off, and she raced past, only a stone's throw from our plodding tramp, her high masts and two tall stacks towering above us. We returned to the rail and watched the silhouettes of the passengers against the bright windows and doors. The strains of a tango came faintly through the night. Once again, death had brushed our ship with its cold breath.

To my great disappointment we passed mighty Gibraltar during the hours of darkness, but even so, the Rock presented an impressive sight, looming black against the sky.

Now the voyage, and life, became pure joy as the balmy air and smooth, blue sea combined to present the picture postcard Mediterranean Sea. Shoes came off, then shirts, until everyone but the captain had stripped to the minimum.

The morning after we passed Gibraltar, as I was walking briskly aft with the breakfast pans, two dirty, unshaven men stepped from behind the mast between the hatches. The older of the two grinned at me, then nodded toward the pans.

"Better set a couple more places," he suggested and headed for the bridge, followed by his companion.

I stared after the stowaways, then slowly continued on my way. The eight o'clock watch had barely left when the two men appeared in our quarters and unceremoniously sat down at the long table. But before they had taken their first sip of coffee, the third mate came in and jerked his thumb toward the sailors' quarters.

"In there," he said curtly and stepped aside.

The stowaways shrugged, winked at me and left.

I was glad, because two more men meant more dirty dishes, more marks on the bulkheads, more water to fetch, more potatoes to peel. Later in the day I learned that Captain Helms, after consigning them to the lowest corner of hell on their demise, had relented and agreed to take them to Shanghai in exchange for their labor. Once there, they could go their own way. Quite unlike today, a man risked little by walking off a ship in an Oriental port provided he kept to himself and out of trouble. I had no inkling that soon I would gain personal knowledge of this.

3

Suez

We arrived in Oran, Algeria, shortly before noon. Our stay was brief, just long enough to discharge a few tons of general cargo and replenish our bunkers. Unable to obtain shoreleave I contented myself, after washing the dishes, by gazing at the gleaming city. I use "gleaming" in its true sense, for under the glaring sun the whitewashed, flat-roofed buildings and slender minarets reflected so much light my eyes soon grew weary from squinting. But it was my first glimpse of the fabled Near East, my first contact with another race, and my heart beat high as I looked at the white city and inhaled the strange, pungent odors which came on the wings of a mild breeze. On a nearby hillside an ebony-black Legionnaire was digging a trench. He was the blackest man I have ever seen. Bare to the waist, his skin, glistening with sweat, reflected brightly in the harsh light of the sun. In the years

The Islands of the Sulu Sea

ahead I would see countless dark men, but never again one so huge and muscular — and so black.

The offshore side of the ship was lined with bumboats. But with Port Said only a few days away, business transactions were few and small, consisting mainly of oranges, and small vials containing the blue-green remains of large flies. My fellow crewmembers quickly and gleefully instructed me in the use of this strange powder. According to some of them, the amount of Spanish Fly one gave depended on the degree of womanly passion desired. But there were others, more skeptical, who loudly insisted that such erotic powers were highly overrated if, indeed, they existed at all. Thus, between the two equally vociferous factions, I learned exactly nothing.

We sailed at sunset. With the coming of the night, the light wind died, leaving the breath of the city laying like a hot blanket. The breeze fanned up by the ship's passage felt luxurious. The night was glorious, with a half moon riding serenely on fluffy clouds.

But when I went on deck at dawn, the sky was grey and the wind had come up. There was nothing left of the travel-folder Mediterranean. Wave after wave rammed the ship abeam, often deluging even the bridge with foamy spray. In a short time even the hot funnel was quickly covered with a coat of salt. I learned the Mediterranean Sea is small and shallow as seas go. Although the waves reached alarming heights, they lacked the punch and power of ocean waves with a fetch of thousands of miles. Thus our ship, while drenched from stem to stern, was rock-steady, a fact which pleased — and relieved — me mightily.

At my low wages, many of the exotic wares of the East would have been beyond my resources but for a timely hint about coffee. From the deck boy, my counterpart in the sailors' quarters, I learned that barter was one way by which merchandise might be obtained in the Orient. He further explained that coffee was the article most likely to find favor.

Milk, bread, cheese, sausage and coffee were rationed on German ships. The coffee was pressed into squares, each three-quarter inch square making a six-cup pot. By simply leaving the grounds in the pot, I soon found that one square made nine cups. Consequently, my private hoard of compressed coffee was a fair-sized pile by the time we arrived at Port Said, Egypt.

Viewed from the ship, Port Said appeared even more intriguing than I anticipated. Even before the anchor chain was tight, a horde of bumboats, manned by hook-nosed, red-fezed, half-naked Muslims, surrounded the ship. My delight knew no bounds as I stood on the poop and stared, awestruck, at the colorful flotilla below.

Only one vendor, an obese, profusely sweating Egyptian was, by what virtue I knew not, permitted on board. Within minutes hatch number five blossomed into a veritable garden of colors. It may have been mostly junk, but it dazzled me as I walked slowly to and fro beside the hatch, unable to tear my eyes from the wondrous display. I had no money, but my left trouser pocket bulged with coffee squares. How much coffee, I wondered, for a pair of camel-hair slippers? A golden bracelet? A jewel encrusted scimitar? A water pipe? Or, closer to the edge of the hatch, a tin of diced pineapple, a box of dates? I fingered my coffee and dismissed the slippers and bracelet and scimitar. No coffee would buy such treasure. But the canned pineapple! I had never tasted pineapple but heard much about its succulence. Licking my lips, I surreptitiously pulled a coffee square from my pocket. Careful not to let my shipmates see, I cupped the coffee in my left hand and hesitantly held it toward the trader, pointing to the small stack of tins. The fat one's eyes rolled knowingly toward other crewmembers; then he smirked and held up five short, be-ringed fingers. My heart sank. Five precious squares for a single can of pineapple, a small, flat can at that. But I could no more have turned away than I could have stopped breath ing. So I fished four more crumbling squares from my pocket and, a moment later, I was on my way, clutching the gaudily papered can.

A few minutes of utter bliss and I licked the last syrupy drop from the yellowish can and tossed it through a porthole. After carefully stowing the remainder of the coffee hoard in my locker, I returned to the deck. There would be more ports and, hopefully, not such expensive ones.

As I emerged, blinking in the hard sunlight, a skinny, elderly Egyptian thrust a piece of paper at me. Turning my back to the sun, I read the message. It was in German and bore no signature. It said:

"This is Mohammed Ali. He is a thief, he is lazy and has syphilis. Also he spits into the dishwater."

I returned the note to the grinning Ali, being careful not to touch his claw-like hand. He said something in English, which I did not understand. A passing sailor, who stopped and read over my shoulder, interrupted.

"He's asking to wash the dishes and clean up for you until we get to Suez — for one German mark."

I stared at him. "B-but the letter. It says that he..."

The sailor laughed. "Somebody's trying to be funny. He knew the poor ape can't read German. It's supposed to be a recommendation." He eyed me keenly. "Will you take him?"

I shook my head no, thinking of the unattainable treasures on the hatch.

The sailor pushed Ali away and said curtly, "No like."

The Egyptian wrung his hands and rolled his eyes heavenward, but when he saw no response, shrugged and turned away.

Passing hatch number five on my way to the foredeck a postcard display caught my eye. Half a dozen picture cards, spread in the shape of a fan were displayed on the hatch cover. My sister would be pleased to receive a greeting from a foreign land. Hastening below, I rummaged in my locker.

The Islands of the Sulu Sea

There I found seven coppers, and determined that they should buy a card. To my surprise the trader nodded as I held my open palm with its seven pfennigs toward him, at the same time gesturing at a picture of the pyramids. Back in our quarters I wrote a greeting on the space provided. One of the firemen gave me a stamp. Then I made an appalling discovery. In the center of the card, between the spaces for address and message, were the words, "Printed in Germany!" Instantly the card lost its romantic appeal. Certain that Gretel would hardly appreciate receiving something that came from Germany in the first place, I carefully scraped the offending letters off with a sharp knife. Then, satisfied that the card's exotic value was restored, I trotted midships and dropped it into the box which the ship's agent would take ashore.

Continuing my interrupted way, I arrived on the foredeck and watched a crew of raggedly-dressed Egyptians manhandle a huge searchlight into position as close to the bow as was possible. A steam generator came next and was placed between the anchor chains. Approaching the third engineer, who was coupling a steam hose to a valve on the anchor winch, I asked the reason for the light. He informed me, quite curtly because he had just skinned his knuckles, that the light was for the night transit through the canal, what else?

The sun was sinking behind the flat roofs on our starboard side when the ship chandler, having deposited the ordered stores outside the storeroom, climbed down the ladder. We cast off from our buoy and were soon gliding slowly past de Lessep's huge statue and into the canal. For awhile a camel-mounted policeman rolled and pitched along the road beside the canal but was soon left behind. I hurried through the supper dishes, then went on deck. The trader was still sitting on the hatch, open for business. But at sunset his men threw a red rug over the merchandise. Then, facing forward, which was also the direction of Mecca, the fat trader and his assistants prostrated themselves on small rugs atop the hatch. At the same time, however, they kept a wary eye on the goods, for a few crew members still lingered nearby.

Night came swiftly, and with it a luxurious coolness. I stood at the taffrail, gazing at the dark, silent land and let my thoughts soar into the past, unfettered by time and space. I thought of Cleopatra, and the Pharaohs who once ruled the land of Isis and Ra and Amon. I thought of Scheherazade and Ali Baba, of caliphs and emirs. My heartbeat increased in step with my thoughts. To my right the land was nearly flat, broken only by an occasional clump of palms or a low hill outlined against the sky. On the left, small flickering fires dotted the desert and I wondered about the people who existed in that dry, sandy wilderness. Oh, how my mind ranged that night. At last, overcome by emotion, I ran below, got a pencil and paper and returned to the poop. There, by the rays from the sternlight, I began to write, inspired by my thoughts and surroundings. At that instant, the firemen blew the boiler tubes. The first inkling I had was a bit of soot, the size of a snow flake landing on my paper. A freak draft from some hot desert valley pressed the column of black smoke downward, sweeping the poop, me, my paper and my inspired thoughts with a blizzard of soot and cinders. Suddenly, the romance was gone and, disgusted, I went to bed.

I was barely asleep when I felt a hand on my arm. The only light came from a single bulb which, like the eternal flame, always burned in the center of the room. In its weak glow I recognized one of the trader's helpers. He beckoned me to move closer to the light. Sliding off the bunk I followed. After a quick, furtive glance around, he pulled a package of cards from under his long robe and thrust it into my hand. I gulped as my eyes fell on the lewd photographs and quickly handed them back. He leered, nodding and smacking his lips. Shaking my head, I climbed back into my bunk and shut my eyes tightly. When I looked again, the purveyor of pornography was gone.

4

The Indian Ocean

Suez was a disappointment, at least as far as the view was concerned. We were glad to be under way again, once the searchlight and generator were removed. The ten-knot breeze stirred up by the ship's passage was a welcome relief from the heat. But, a day out of Suez, a light westerly wind suddenly plunged us into a veritable furnace. Keeping apace with the ship, the breeze, a boon for westbound traffic, put us into a total calm. We were covered by a fiery, suffocating blanket that made breathing a torture and sent rivulets of sweat coursing over our bodies at the slightest exertion. A heavy column of smoke from the funnel hung over the ship like a pall, dropping flakes of soot, adding to our misery. With the onset of warm weather I stowed my wooden clogs and went barefoot. Now I broke them out again, for the deckplates were so hot that no foot, however calloused, could remain unblistered. The direct rays of the brassy sun, their reflections from the sea, the heated decks, the total absence of a breeze made life almost unbearable. The heat <u>was</u> unbearable in the engine and boiler rooms, where the atmosphere was absolutely infernal. This was especially true before the change of the watch. It was then the furnace doors were thrown open while glowing slag was raked onto the deck. Here one caught a truly vivid glimpse of hell — the yellow-red flames lashing from the openings, the piles of flickering smoking slag on the deck, the wraith-like forms of the panting firemen working their heavy sluice bars around the lurid maws of the great furnaces. When all was done and the watch at an end, the men stumbled up the hot ladders into a slightly less scorched atmosphere. Here and there a haggard, hollow-eyed engineman writhed on the deck until his stomach cramps abated long enough for him to stagger to his bunk, where he lay, panting and sick, on a sweat-soaked straw mattress.

Lime juice, the one unrationed item, was drunk in prodigious quantities, and in consequence I was horrified one afternoon to find the bottle empty. The storeroom didn't open until five o'clock, and the watch would be coming in, tired, exhausted and thirsty at four. If they didn't find their accustomed lime juice... I had felt the sting of horned hands before and had no wish to repeat the experience. Frantically I searched the various bunks for a hidden bottle, but in vain. Then I had an inspiration. Filling a bottle half full with weak coffee, I sloshed the contents vigorously, in the faint hope that a few drops from the sides would lend the coffee at least a sourish taste. Then I sampled it. It took all the imagination I could muster to taste any sourness at all, but there was nothing I could do, particularly since at that moment I heard the shuffling of tired feet overhead. Quickly, I poured the "juice" into a cup and looked at it. It was a little dark but <u>could be</u> the real thing, especially since it came from a dark green lime juice bottle. When the first man entered I retreated to a far corner. One by one the weary men filled their cups with tepid water, added generous slugs of "lime juice," a

The "black gang" or engine crew of the Eta Rickmers. *That's me on the lower right. From the author's collection.*

little sugar, and drank long and deeply. Not one man noticed anything amiss and soon the bottle was empty, the incriminating evidence gone. I was the first one at the storeroom at five o'clock.

For five full days the trial by fire plagued us, and it was only after we cleared the Strait of Bab el Mandeb and were cresting the slow swell of the Indian Ocean that life became pleasant once more. I was told the Indian Ocean has only two moods: violently wild or extraordinarily serene. I know nothing of the former, but can fully vouch for the latter. One radiant day followed the other. But the nights are what linger in my memory like a pleasant dream. Deep black after the moon set and sparkling with stars so near and bright that I seemed to be in another world. I lay for hours on the cool hatch covers, watching the mast circle lazily among the glittering constellations. Living was pure joy during those tranquil days and jewel-studded nights. The happiness was reflected in the happy expressions on the weather-beaten faces around me, in the banter, the easy laughter, the good humor. It was on such a night, as the ship plodded slowly along like a contented cow over a gently rolling meadow, that we were startled from sleep by a sharp jolt followed by a soft scraping. Everyone rushed on deck. The moon was down and the darkness thick. Running to the rail we stared into the blue-green phosphorescence brought up from the deep by the whirling screw. All was quiet save the subdued hiss of the wide wake. What had we struck? A whale? A derelict? One of the numerous boats which ply the Indian Ocean? Like all men of the sea I would, in the years ahead, hear and read of collisions at sea, but none was more poignant than that of the steamer which had run down a schooner in the Bay of Bengal. The young third mate was absolved of blame; human eyes and ears are far from perfect. But afterward, his shipmates found him sitting alone in a small waterfront cafe, his untouched food cold on the plate. Yes, he'd been found blameless. But he would never sail again. It was not the sight of that spectral hull looming suddenly from the darkness which unnerved him, nor yet the shock of impact, nor the sound of the scraping and the splintering along the stout plates. Those were sights and sounds a man could cope with -- and forget. It was the cry of that child, out there in the abject darkness, that cry of terror and despair, and the silence afterward, more eloquent than the cry, which followed him through the night and would go with him to the grave.

But on that night we heard nothing, no cry, only the thud and the soft scraping. Behind us the sea lifted and fell rhythmically, our secret forever locked in her deep.

Only once did we glimpse the other mood of the great Indian Ocean, in the form of three huge waterspouts marching across the horizon ten miles away, three twisting funnels of fury, churning the water below and the clouds above.

An hour later a windjammer hove into view off our starboard bow, bound, no doubt, for England from Australia on one of the last great grain races. It was a never-to-be-forgotten sight, that graceful vessel on the azure sea, its billowing sails matching the white clouds in the blue sky. I looked the length of our steamer. How ungainly she must appear from the distance, I thought, how clumsy, plowing into the swells at a bare ten knots instead of all but flying like the clipper a few miles away. But then, you simply cannot compare a squat tramp steamer with a full-rigged ship with all sails drawing, anymore than you can compare a duck to a swan.

A day out of Colombo, Ceylon, my idyl was abruptly and painfully shattered. Carrying two buckets of near-boiling water aft, my left foot slipped off its wooden clog. Losing my balance, I set the buckets down, at the same time plunging both arms to the elbows in the scalding water. There was no pain, but I knew that it would not be long in coming. Continuing aft, I deposited the almost empty buckets in the washroom and hurriedly walked forward. The pain, hastened by the hot sun, was rapidly mounting. Our doctor, only recently graduated, poured alcohol over my arms; then applied a salve and bandaged the arms from elbow to fingertips. For a while the pain subsided, but by the time the bandages were on and I stepped on deck, the burning became excruciating. When we entered Colombo harbor at noon the following day and the light breeze died, the agony was intense. I walked for hours on end around the auxiliary steering wheel on the poop, only vaguely aware of the curious stares of the Ceylonese stevedores and traders who swarmed over the ship. Huge blisters rose on my arms and hands, forcing the bandages apart, revealing the raw flesh underneath. Twice each day the doctor slit the heavy bubbles to drain the water, bringing additional torment as the air entered the collapsed blisters. I did no work that week. When I tried to work it was a disaster. Lifting a pan of pea soup onto the table with stiff arms, I accidentally overturned it, drenching my messmates.

By the time we reached the tip of Sumatra and entered the Strait of Mallaca, I recovered sufficiently to enjoy life again. I spent every free minute at the starboard rail staring raptly at the jungles of the green islands, conjuring up fantastic visions of wildlife and barbaric men.

At the mouth of the Strait, the ship behaved in an extraordinary manner, yawing and twisting alarmingly, seemingly bent on bucking free of the restraining hands on the wheel. The surface of the sea was a patchwork of glassy calm and wave-lashed wilderness. When the steamer crossed such a patch, the water would be perfectly smooth on one side, while the breakers leaped aboard on the other. Once inside the Strait, however, she settled down once more, answering the helm in a most docile manner.

We arrived at Singapore, one degree south of the Equator, at two in the morning. Despite the lateness of the hour I was on deck drinking in the sight of — what? It mattered little. What mattered was that I was gazing at Singapore, in the heart of the mysterious East. As if to emphasize this fact, the red sickle of the late moon rose over the city, silhouetting waterfront shed and pagoda alike.

Our anchor had barely dug into the mud outside the harbor when the agent's white launch — agents always, it seemed, had white launches — roared out of the night and made fast at the hastily lowered gangway. A half hour later, those who remained awake received their long-awaited letters. Singapore, after Port Said, was one of the few ports where mail could be sent. The others were Manila, Hong Kong, Shanghai, Kobe, Japan and Vladivostok, Russia.

Due to the nature of our cargo, the ship was not permitted to enter the inner harbor. At the first light of dawn, lighters made fast on both sides of the ship, and the unloading began. It lasted the entire day. When it was done and the hatches battened down, a deeply laden coal barge came alongside and was made fast amidships. Throughout the hot, humid night the stillness was broken by the dull thud and whoosh of coal dropping into the bunkers. It came from a hundred baskets on the muscular shoulders of a hundred near-naked sweating coolies trooping up one swaying plank and down another, a hundred glistening bodies, which grew blacker and wearier as the long night wore on. With the coming of the day the barge was empty, swept clean of the last lump of coal, and a hundred dusty, sweaty, utterly exhausted bodies dropped to the black deck.

We took on coal and stores, but no water. At my puzzled question, for I knew that our water supply was low, I was told of two standard procedures on German ships, and most likely ships of other nations, on the Far East run. Number One: Try to make your water last until arrival at Manila. Number Two: Keep your laundry for Hong Kong. The first was explained promptly. Manila water was extraordinarily soft and pure, a virtue much appreciated by the engineers of steamers and diesel ships alike. Number two, I was assured, with a leer, would answer itself in Hong Kong.

The approximate route of the Eta Rickmers *is traced on this world map along*

The Islands of the Sulu Sea

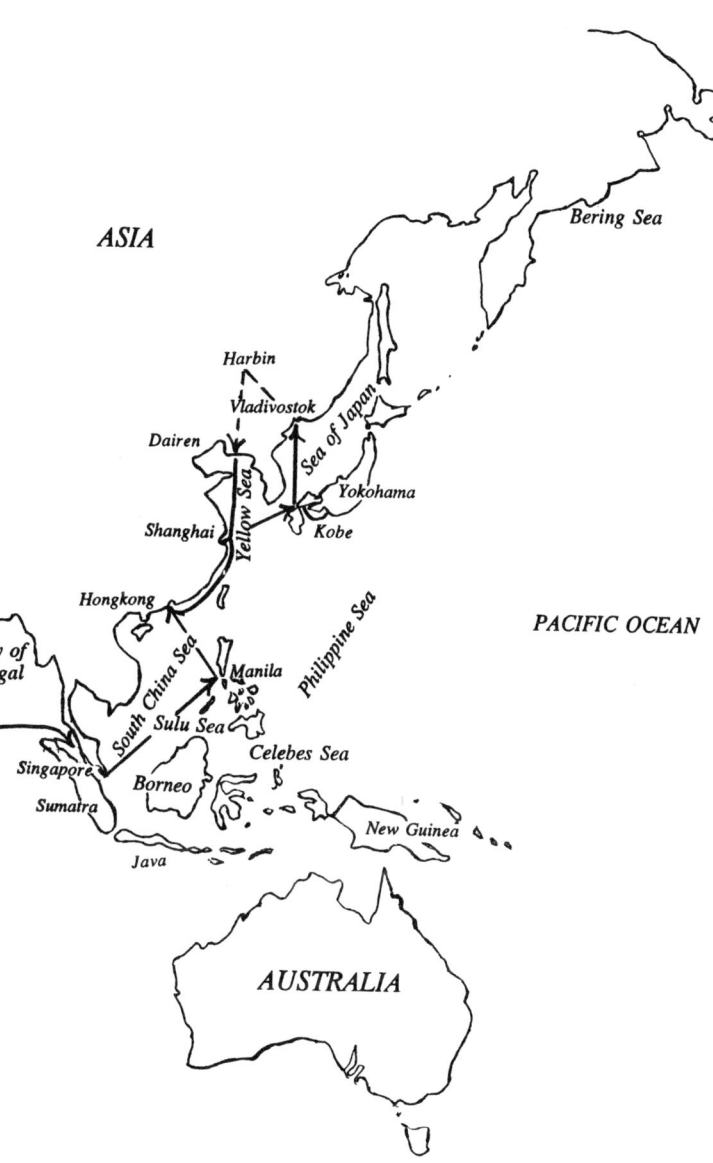

with some of my subsequent travels both by land and by sea in the Far East.

5

Manila, the First Time

We departed Singapore in mid-morning and were soon bucking the swell of the South China Sea. Course: Northeast. Destination: Manila, the Philippines. At about noon the next day, a much awaited sight, for me, came into view. Far to the south, off the starboard bow, loomed Borneo. Of all the islands on this earth Borneo, for no reason whatsoever, had the greatest appeal for me. It still has. I saw little of it that day, a dark hump on the horizon, but what my eyes could not see, my imagination revealed with startling clarity; and even as my body leaned against the rail, my spirit roamed the huge island, across mountain ranges, through steaming rain forests, over miasmatic swamps, inside the longhouses of fierce headhunters.

The island had long sunk beneath the horizon when, at last, and quite reluctantly, I recalled my wandering spirit and went below. Little did I know that sunlit day that within a year and a half I would stand upon Borneo's wild shores. Nor did I ever dream I would feel at home on the surrounding waters of the Sulu Sea.

We entered Manila Bay during the most spectacular sunset I had ever seen. I later learned that extravagant sunsets are the rule in the Bay of Manila. To our right, above a high ridge, towered a mass of golden clouds, a veritable city of light with pillars and columns of pink and mauve, with shady portals and lofty arches; and lower, the ramparts and spires of a formidable bastion. But even as I watched, open mouthed, the scene changed as the sun disappeared behind the mountains of the peninsula on our left. Where only moments before had stood a city, ethereal and shimmering, a cauldron of fire began to boil. The stately pillars melted; the lofty arches sunk and fell; the mighty ramparts crumbled and collapsed amid the lurid glare like at the mouth of hell. And in the midst of that flaming, swirling mass moved grey, misty wisps of cloud like the restless souls of the damned. The calm sea mirrored the flaming sky, and the steamer seemed to plow a furrow of liquid fire. All too soon nothing was left of the spectacle but a grey, misshapen lump of cloud above the land. And, high up, a long finger of zodiacal light touched the almost dark sky with a final caress.

A dim glow ahead announced the distant city, brightened perceptibly, then resolved itself into myriad separate lights. Manila. Again, I had no inkling that in less than two months the bright city before me would become my virtual hometown and would remain so for more than twenty years. As it was, I stood on the foredeck, enthralled by the lights, excited at the thought of shoreleave. For at Manila I would step ashore in the Orient for the first time, ten thousand miles and forty days from home.

We anchored a mile from the breakwater, one of several ships which had arrived too late for clearance.

The Islands of the Sulu Sea

At nine-thirty the next morning, our yellow quarantine flag came down, the red and white pilot flag went up, and we proceeded at slow speed into the harbor, anchoring just off the fairway near the breakwater.

That evening I hurried through the supper dishes, and when the checkered water taxi tied up at the gangway, I was there. All spruced up, with a ten peso bill and a package of prophylactics in my pocket, the latter item issued at the gangway by the fourth officer, I was ready for the mysteries of the Orient. In the company of several of my shipmates, I climbed the concrete steps between piers 3 and 5 a few minutes later. After so many days at sea, the firm land was difficult to walk on. The ground seemed to be rolling alarmingly, and I had to make a definite effort not to flex my knees in concert with the apparent motion underfoot.

Since I had not visited Manila before, I thought it prudent to attach myself to Hans, my counterpart in the sailors' quarters. In addition to having been there before, he spoke English of a sort (I spoke none).

The wide street outside the pier was deserted except for a few carriages. Consisting of a two-seat cab sitting on leaf springs above two high wheels, and drawn by a small, high-spirited pony, these served as taxis. We decided to live it up and signalled one. The driver removed the guard, clicked his tongue, and we were off at a fast trot. I leaned back, smiling

The Islands of the Sulu Sea

to myself. If my folks could see me now, they whose horizons were so limited, whose lives were so utterly dreary. We rode up one broad boulevard after another, past the wide, dry moat that surrounds the old Walled City, over a steel girdered bridge, into the heart of the city. There I paid the fare and we sauntered up and down the Avenida Rizal, Manila's main thoroughfare. At Hans' behest we also walked through several alleys where brazen and scantily-clad girls disported themselves in a most unbecoming manner. To my relief, for I was a bit uncomfortable in that strange atmosphere, I saw a few familiar objects, buses, streetcars, taxicabs. Familiar, yet different, for they all drove on the left side of the street; their signals were different, as were their colors, and the trams stopped at every corner, an unheard-of procedure in super-efficient Germany. There was much to see, so much, in fact that I retained little in my memory. But I knew no better, and the mere realization that I walked along the streets of an Oriental city was enough to put me in a state of bliss.

At 8 p.m. we sat in the front row of the Savoy, a small, shoddy theater on the Plaza Santa Cruz directly across from a massive, fort-like church. The movie was titled "Stark Mad." I recognized only the word "stark," and that mistakenly, for in German stark means strong, robust. But whereas the dialogue was Greek to me, the scenes were interesting. After the film came a stage show. I could not understand a single word, but the tunes were lovely and haunting, as were the tawny, swinging limbs of the lissome girls above us. After it was over, my friend, more mature than I and, possibly more affected by forty days of abstinence and the sight of lightly-clad chorus girls, proposed that we re-visit one of the narrow alleys in search of pleasure. I demurred, and outside the Savoy we parted, he adventure bent, I for a leisurely stroll to the harbor where a boat would be waiting just after midnight.

I sauntered down the narrow Escolta, Manila's diminutive Fifth Avenue, with its fashionable shops, its banks, its restaurants. On the long sweeping arch of Jones Bridge I halted and gazed at the black, slow-flowing water of the Pasig, the river which, like the Elbe, the Thames, and the Seine divides a great city. A tugboat with two barges in tow crawled upstream, past a long line of inter-island steamers moored to the cobblestone quay on the north bank. Huge islands of white and purple water hyacinths floated toward the sea. Farther downstream, two flashing white lights marked the mouth of the river. Continuing my leisurely way, I walked across a wide, grassy plaza, enveloped in the heavy fragrance of night flowers, and down broad Avenida Taft.

The night was still and balmy and utterly enchanting. At a new, many-columned building I turned right into a narrow street spanning a grassy moat, and stepped from the Twentieth Century into the Nineteenth. The streets of the Walled City were narrow, cobblestoned, and dirty. The thick-walled houses were two and sometimes three-storied affairs with large windows upstairs, and smaller, heavily-barred ones on the ground floor. Balconies ran the entire length of some houses, and were occupied here and there by elderly, often fat women sitting in rocking chairs, slowly rocking and fanning themselves in the hot night air. The measured clip-clop of pony hoofs echoed hollowly from the stone walls. American policemen in khaki uniforms and cork helmets patrolled the streets. I walked slowly, very slowly, stopping frequently to gape at the occupants of a passing carriage, often obese Chinese, less frequently a pair of laughing Filipinas, and once, a beauteous Spanish girl in company of a sharp-nosed elderly woman who spoke angrily to the girl. It was almost midnight when I reached the end of the half-mile long alley, and stepped through the thick, arched gate back into the Twentieth Century. A few minutes' walk along an avenue of lofty palms brought me to the harbor.

Twice more, in the four days of our stay, I went ashore, becoming ever more charmed with that gracious city.

6

Shanghai

We sailed into a glowering sunset. Three days later, the first Chinese junk, a clumsy, down-by-the-head craft with fantastically patched sails, hove into sight. Once again I stood, agog, by the taffrail as the junk, a microcosm itself, careened across our wake. That night, a call from Hans brought me on deck in a hurry. He stood at the port rail, pointing ahead. The ship was heading directly for a line of bright lights.

"Hong Kong?" I asked innocently.

"You'll see."

Abruptly the steady beat of the propeller slowed, and presently the ship was in the center of a great fleet of small fishing junks, each with a brilliant light suspended over the side. We threaded our way through the fleet at a dead-slow pace to the accompaniment of sing-song shouts, curses, and shaking fists.

I found Hong Kong to be the exact opposite of Manila, noisy, lively, garish, wholly lacking the serene grace of the Philippine capital. Even from our vantage point in midstream the anthill comparison was evident. This feverish activity has always been the trademark of Hong Kong — the "Fragrant Harbor." When we stepped ashore that evening dodging buses, rickshaws, streetcars and pole-swinging peddlers, my first impression was one of noise. It dogged us, assaulted us from the front, from the sides, from above. The click of mahjongg tiles from behind shuttered windows, the shouts of hawkers, the sudden rataplan of fireworks kept me constantly on edge. At one particularly cacophonous whine of Cantonese-or-whatever-type "music", as we passed a gaudily illuminated, poster-plastered dance hall, I couldn't help wincing. But I was in China, at last, fabled China, and I was determined that nothing would be allowed to mar the few hours I would spend ashore. The women were alluring, not only the slender maids in the tight, high-slitted dresses, but the sampan girls as well, in their black pants, their loose blouses, their conical hats tied with a ribbon under the chin.

Again my friend Hans deserted me at the sight of a young, well-endowed and brazen Chinese temptress. After failing, just barely, to convince me that at my age — well, he failed, and in another moment he was gone, swallowed by a nearby door.

I entered a cinema and sat through a war film. At the end, the audience rose while an unseen band played a somewhat martial air. I stood too, wondering why a theater in a British Crown Colony should play a German anthem. I have heard the tune often, since. It was "God Save the King."

As in Manila, I walked slowly to the harbor, along the still-crowded streets, under red and gold banners, past money changers, around fawning merchants, away from imploring

The Islands of the Sulu Sea

beggars, avoiding leering procurers. The waterfront was quiet and quite devoid of traffic except for an occasional rickshaw or taxi. The godown doors looked shadowy and eerie and my pace quickened. The atmosphere was suddenly dark and forbidding. But Fu Man Chu's henchmen did not materialize to abduct me; no tall, thin, evil-faced Mandarin bade me trot behind his rickshaw. Just the same, I felt a hearty relief when I spotted a big, bearded Sikh policeman on the quay. I resolved right there to walk alone no more in the East, a resolution that would be completely thrown aside in less than a month.

Back on board, I stopped at the rail and gazed at the city. It was a beautiful scene — the brilliant mass of many-colored lights in the foreground, the winking, shimmering pinpoints on the hill and their glittering counterparts in the black sky beyond. It reminded me of a great jewel suspended in space.

We remained in Hong Kong for three days during which I learned many things. A man could have himself measured for a suit at 5 p.m. and wear it the next morning. I learned that gold was cheap in Hong Kong, not that it did me any good. I also learned that as many as four generations live aboard a junk, were conceived, born, grew up, and died on the water. But long before all that, in fact, within an hour after our arrival, I had learned why the laundry was always kept until Hong Kong. As I watched, incredulously, and not a little embarrassedly, the sailors and firemen thrust bundles of soiled clothes at the comely, pig-tailed girls, then led them into the spare cubicles adjacent to the washrooms. The girls, you see, did more than merely wash the clothes — and all included in one low fee.

When I finished admiring the jeweled sky that first night, I walked forward to number one hatch where the dynamite was being discharged into a junk. When I arrived, I noticed a great ado, for the junk had sprung a leak and was sinking. Already, the single hatch was flooded, and sing-song pleas and curses flew in abundance. The few sailors on watch finally succeeded in looping two cables under the junk and making them fast to the bitts, thus preventing the craft from sinking entirely. As the cases of dynamite were hurriedly returned to the ship, one case fell from its pallet and broke apart, strewing the wet sticks around the deck. I picked one up and headed for our quarters. There, I carefully peeled the wrapper off and laid the stick on the stove to dry. It was just beginning to hiss and sizzle when someone walked into the room and, roaring with anger and alarm, flung the smoking stick of dynamite through the porthole. He then made certain that I would never again place explosives on a hot stove.

We made Woosung, at the mouth of the Yangtze Kiang, early in the morning of a dreary day and immediately proceeded to unload the remaining dynamite and blasting caps into barges. On our return from Shanghai, we would then reload the explosives. The moment we anchored the ship was flooded with customs officials and tradesmen: tailors, shoemakers, barbers, dentists. Seeing my chipped front tooth, one of the dentists persuaded me, via my friend Hans, that my chances with the ladies, particularly Chinese, would be vastly improved were I to have my tooth repaired and suitably framed in gold, for eight dollars, Chinese. I agreed, and a half hour later, the dentist departed, my tooth imprint and four dollars in his pocket, leaving me only the promise to have the inlay ready by the time we reached Shanghai the following morning. He kept his word. By 9 a.m., after a little filing and sandpapering, my tooth was whole once more, and rimmed in shiny gold.

The harbor of Shanghai was in the river, wide and muddy. No piers stuck out, but both banks were lined with concrete quays. Buoys in midstream held the ships that could not be accommodated at the wharfs.

Again I walked along broad streets and narrow alleys, aware of the somewhat familiar sights and smells. Only I did not go alone. When Hans, as usual, became restless and instinctively headed for a certain district, I went along. But when we returned to the ship at dawn, I was almost ill with worry, despite the precautions taken. And disease did indeed strike. A fireman and two trimmers came down with venereal afflictions, contracted, probably from the Hong Kong girls. The sailors fared no better. Two were infected. But, strangely, nothing was done to isolate the sick men. They were allowed to live in the cramped quarters, keeping only their eating gear apart and receiving an occasional neo-salvarsan injection. They did their work uncomplainingly even when they could barely walk. I was terrified and promised myself to confine my shore leave to sightseeing.

I quickly came to regard Shanghai as a huge den of vice and debauchery, of rape and murder, a veritable cesspool of evil. The Bund, a long, wide, bank-and-businesshouse-lined boulevard along the waterfront, looked respectable enough, and even the narrow alleys of the great city appeared harmless in the daytime. It was at nightfall that the city changed. Then the alleys swarmed with furtive, vice-bent men of all races. It was then that the traffic in human bodies began, from the lowly Chinese girl at four dollars, Shanghai, a night, in some bedbug-ridden cubicle along the Soochow Creek, to the haughty, white courtesan in her swank flat in the French Concession at a hundred dollars. In later years I would see the less squalid side of Shanghai, but during the five days we lay there I saw and heard little beyond sex, opium and disease, as otherwise staid family men anxiously awaited the coming of the night with its orgies of lust and drugs.

Our next port was Tsing-wan-tao in North China, then Chinampo, and Chimulpo off the coast of Korea, each of these without docks and no shore leave. They left no impression on my memory save there seemed to be a superabundance of eggs that were the main produce of the region. Then followed a bewildering succession of ports in Japan: Kobe,

The Islands of the Sulu Sea

Nagasaki, Moji, Shimonoseki, Nagoya, Yokohama. In no port did we remain more than twenty-four hours except Yokohama, where the first person on board after the customs inspectors was a personable young European woman with sparkling blue eyes and pink cheeks who stood at the gangway, handing little cards to the passers-by. I had no trouble deciphering the heading, "Yokohama Seaman's Mission." Hans translated the rest, "Services 8 p.m. nightly. Refreshments served. All are welcome."

Hans and I went ashore that night. I was somewhat surprised to hear him propose a visit to the mission. Whether it was a sudden desire on his part for a more wholesome atmosphere after his escapades at Manila and the other ports, or just plain fear of the consequences, or even guilt, I don't know. For my part, I was glad enough to go because of the promised refreshments. I had no sense of guilt, or fear of divine retribution, for my atheist father had taught me well. I bought a few yards of blue silk for my sister, then we took a streetcar to the approximate vicinity of the mission. As we walked slowly along narrow streets, I asked about the red lights that glowed above some doors, and was duly instructed on their meaning. I wondered aloud what a mission was doing in a district given over to the satisfying of carnal desires. Hans pointed out that it was a Seaman's Mission.

Where, he asked with light sarcasm, were seamen usually found?

The people at the mission, who turned out to be Swedish, were friendly. The talk, translated into German by a young woman, was boring, but the ice cream and the cookies were delicious. On leaving we accepted some religious tracts, which somehow fluttered from our fingers before we had gone two blocks. Twice, as we passed some well-built, peach-skinned girls, my friend's steps faltered, but we reached the ship safely, tempted, but, fortunately, unsatisfied.

7

Alone In Vladivostok

A week's steaming along the east coast of Kyoto and across the Sea of Japan brought us to Vladivostok on Siberia's bleak eastern coast. Little did I suspect that I was about to reach the end of one phase of my young life, and that cold, drab Vladivostok would mean a complete break with the existence I had known.

We remained for several weeks during which our quarters literally swarmed with women, some surprisingly lovely. Every second day the harbor police raided the ship, and any girl not agile enough to escape into the shaft tunnel was hauled to prison, where she would languish a day then reappear, rested and in high spirits the following night. In an atmosphere utterly devoid of morals, it was virtually impossible for a youngster such as myself to sidestep temptations.

The Islands of the Sulu Sea

Ashore we were feted and guided. I was aware that the revolution in Russia a dozen-some years ago had toppled the Czar and knew that socialists -- some called them communists -- maintained the social order. But I had little interest in such things and had no opinion, adverse or otherwise, regarding my present hosts. We visited farms to observe fat and healthy pigs. We saw lumber camps and construction sites, with their neat, airy barracks and Balalaika-playing workers. The Seaman's Club was large and comfortable, the hostesses friendly and cute. We were escorted to an outdoor theater where I fell hopelessly in love with a young singer without even meeting her afterward or ever knowing her name.

On a spur of the moment, I sold the silk I purchased in Japan, not knowing that there was little to buy in Vladivostok. There were only two stores and they were sold out before the long queue was half served, at 4:30 a.m. But the city did have one capitalist and we all wondered how he survived. He was old and Chinese or perhaps Korean. Pushing his cart around the town, he peddled bread, white bread sometimes, cookies, fruits, dried fish.

On the evening before departure, in anticipation of a party at the Club, we went ashore early, so early in fact, that I left the dinner dishes unwashed. The Customs officer at the head of the pier searched us carefully on this our last night in his paradise. We then headed for the Club. The girls (some of them were stevedores) were charming and gay and quite willing to retire to some dim, quiet corner. Language barriers do not exist for a seaman. A little German, a bit of Russian, a word or two in English were enough, and when conversation lagged, a smile, a nod, a light pressure of the hand spoke even more eloquently.

It was past midnight when we said farewell and walked slowly and reluctantly, for the girls had been extraordinarily sweet, to the harbor.

Then I remembered the unwashed dishes. Suddenly I couldn't bear the thought of them. At that instant, as I stopped in the middle of the intersection, my mind in a turmoil, the first phase of my life came to an end. And when I turned into a sidestreet on that cold, wet night, half a world from home, I changed not only my physical course, but that of my future existence as well.

A stack of soiled dishes! Many a life had doubtlessly been altered by trivial things; I claim no distinction in that respect. It was the foolhardiness of my sudden decision that, I daresay, made it unique -- the time, the reason, and, above all, the place, 12,000 miles from home in cold, hostile Siberia. I jumped ship.

Had I had the advice of an older and, therefore, wiser man, the result might have been different, but I was young, very young and alone. Was it really only a stack of dirty dishes? Was it the terrible conditions of post World War I Germany? I thought of the destructive inflation, the unemployment, the hundreds of laid-up ships. Or was it the girl singer on the stage, whom I had not even met? What was behind all this, or who? Those thoughts came later, not on that cold street in the night, and it would be years before I knew.

8

Hitchhiking In Asia

My new life began the moment I entered that dark street -- and how different it was! I no longer had a home, such as it was, waiting for me, no longer anyone to help, to guide, or scold. I was alone. I had enough money to last a week or a little longer. The only hotel was filled, mostly with party functionaries, and there were no rooming houses. Then it began to rain, a cold and very wet rain. Passing a lumber yard I crawled into a stack of boards. It was cold, but at least dry. I spent a miserable night but slept with the coming of the day, waking with a start at the sound of a hoarse whistle blast not far away. Crawling from my hard bed, I squinted at the watery sun. I had no watch, but knew my ship was to sail at 8 a.m. Although I couldn't see it, I recognized the repeated blasts from her whistle, perhaps calling me. Brushing the sawdust from my suit, I ran my stiff fingers through my hair and climbed a low, nearby hill. There, screened from the harbor by bushes, I watched the ship cast off and steam seaward. Abruptly, the magnitude of my foolishness dawned on me and despite the cold I felt my forehead grow moist. What had I done? How long would I last, alone in an alien country, almost broke, ignorant of the language? I fought a wave of sheer terror even as my eyes were glued to the green-hulled ship below. I bit my lip to keep it from trembling. Watching until the steamer had disappeared behind the headland, I was relieved to find that with its disappearance my spirit lifted. I took a deep breath and headed for the town.

Having no plans, I walked aimlessly about as day followed dreary day. I slept where I could, once even huddling in a group of fur-clad peasants who awaited the early train to Sakhalin and had bedded down on the cold ground outside the locked railroad station. It was smelly among their thick furs but warm. I bought my bread from the street vendor, had an occasional cup of hot tea in the tea room, and washed my face in a creek outside the town.

Without the smiling, affable guides, I saw the real Russia, with its naked misery and filth. If I had any illusions about the vaunted workers' paradise, they were quickly shattered on the first day.

On one of my wanderings around the city I climbed a low hill, attracted by the number of ventilators on top. As I was peering into one after the other, a man appeared with two large hounds. He said something, which I did not understand, and left. When I reached the bottom I noticed, set in a recess of the hill, a large metal door. I later learned it was an ammunition depot, but at the time thought nothing of it and continued my wandering. It was cold and passing a tall building, I decided to look for a warm place there and rest or even spend the night. The two guards at the entrance smiled and let me enter. On the second floor I saw, through a small window on a door, a number of what appeared to be army men at their desks. I turned swiftly and ran down, but the guards placed their rifles, which I had not noticed on entering, in front of me, and almost immediately two soldiers appeared and took me, one on each side, to what soon appeared to be a prison. The man at the desk frisked me and removed all that was in my pockets, and then a cell door opened. The room was bare save for a long wooden table and a long bench on either side. In one corner was a sort of toilet. Two ill-clad men were already in the room. The table, I discovered, was both for eating and sleeping. No bedding at all. But it was warm and that was what counted. The food was mostly black bread. Five days later, an officer who spoke German returned my few possessions and said I could go, but he suggested that I accept a job on the railroad in central Siberia, but I had heard what that would mean and so I said, "Nyet."

When my capital was reduced to a few rubles, I decided to act and presented myself at the German Consulate. There I was given my first hot meal in nearly two weeks, a bath, and a verbal whipping. Then the consul gave me a sum of money, I forget the amount, and sent me on my way with several instructions. A quarter of the money was in rubles, the rest in yen. Since no German ship was expected at Vladivostok for some time, I was to make my way to Dairen, on the southern tip of Manchuria, where I was to report to the consul there and be shipped home to prison. At that time desertion was punishable by incarceration. I agreed readily (I had no alternative), but with a good deal of mental reservation.

At 9 a.m. on a drizzly April day, sans baggage, I nonchalantly boarded the Trans-Siberian Railroad train. My ticket said Harbin, where I would change trains. The third class coach was quite comfortable, but entering the elegant dining car at noon I suddenly became self-conscious. The tables were spotless. My suit was shabby; not only shabby but also dirty. Hurrying through the meal, I kept my eyes on my plate. I paid for my meal hastily with yen, embarrassed because I seemed to be the focal point of attention, and left the car. Two meals later, we arrived at the border, and to my consternation, my rubles were confiscated. Now I realized my foolishness in spending the Japanese yen and keeping the Russian currency. The consul had figured closely, relying, mistakenly, on my judgment. The amount he gave me, including the rubles, was barely enough to get me to Dairen.

At Harbin I carefully counted my resources and bought a ticket to Mukden, the end of the line for that train. By the window, opposite me, sat a tall, slender Chinese man. He wore the long, black embroidered robe and small cap of a Mandarin. He had long fingernails, gray hair, a wispy beard, and a benign smile which he concentrated on me the moment I sat down. It was the first friendly smile I'd seen in many days. If I were a puppy, I would have wagged my tail. He spoke to me in a soft, sing-song voice. I didn't understand a word he said, but liked the sound. My only reaction was to shake my head and raise my hands, palms up, in the universal "no savvy" gesture. Thereafter, for many miles, his gentle, slanting eyes were on me, and now and then he nodded to himself as if reaching some decision. We left the train together, but I lost him in the crowd. It mattered little to me. I was anxious to continue my journey.

As nearly as I could calculate, I had sufficient money to get to Dairen — if I didn't eat. At my age this was impossible, of course, so, after purchasing a ticket for the next end-of-the-line, I headed for the nearby market and bought a few rice cakes.

I arrived in Tashinkiao in mid-afternoon. Sitting on a bench waiting for the Dairen train, my eyes fell on a large poster. At least a third of it was occupied by the picture of a large ferry boat. Picking out a word here and there — Yingkow to Shanghai; 10 o'clock; Friday — I came to the conclusion that the boat left for Shanghai from Yingkow at

The Islands of the Sulu Sea

10 o'clock on Friday. It said A.M., but since I didn't know what that meant, I ignored it.

For a long time, as I sat on the hard bench, and for the first time, I considered my future. It was appalling. Germany, at the time, vacillated between two equally destructive ideologies, communism and fascism. I had a glimpse of both and liked neither. Add to this the prospect of a prison term for jumping ship, however mild and short, and the outlook was bleak indeed. A little arithmetic assured me that I had just enough money to get to Shanghai. Staring at the boat on the poster, I wondered briefly what I would do in Shanghai, penniless and alone. There was no answer. Dismissing the problem from my mind, I bought a ticket for the city of Yingkow on the Gulf of the same name.

The train evidently connected with the ferry, because we arrived in Yingkow shortly after 9 a.m. But I promptly lost my way. When I finally reached the pier, I saw, to my dismay, the ferry just pulling away. I considered jumping but knew it was hopeless. A good ten yards of yellow water already separated ship from pier.

Walking slowly back to the station, I knew I would never get to Dairen. That futile side trip had done it. When I got back to Tashinkiao I had just enough money for a ticket to Wah-fang-tien, a small station on the Dairen line. I was tired, hungry, and discouraged. But I was also young, and by the time we arrived at Wah-fang-tien, I had slept a little and felt much better. Disembarking, I stood by the tracks and forlornly watched the train leave.

As the next-to-the-last car rolled by, a familiar face suddenly appeared at a window. A pair of slanting, fatherly eyes widened at the sight of me; a thin arm in a wide sleeve beckoned frantically; I could almost hear him shout in his sing-song voice, "Jump on! Join me! Quickly!" Hesitating for an instant, I then raised my arms to grasp the handhold on the last car's rear step. It was too late. The car was gone.

The venerable Mandarin leaned from the window, his wispy beard streaming in the wind, and raised his hand in salute.

Angrily kicking the rail, I started walking along the tracks, morosely wondering how long it would take to walk a hundred miles. But soon my spirits soared again. The day was lovely; spring was at hand. My feeling of joy was short-lived. Toward evening the tracks entered a forest, and as darkness came and the fog closed in, I felt the first vague stirring of fear. How lonesome it was, how silent and ghostly. I longed for the friendly bark of a dog, the sight of a light in a window, the sound of human voices. There was only silence and fog and darkness. Once, as I trudged along the narrow path beside the rails, the stillness was shattered by a long, drawn-out howl close at hand. I stopped, trembling. Wolves! My mouth felt dry. Despite the cold I began sweating, as I stood perfectly still, staring intently into the night. Then, in a pathetic attempt at protection, I picked up two rocks and, stepping softly, walked on.

Around midnight the fog lifted a little and so did my heart. Ahead, at a curve in the tracks was a simple semaphore light. Its weak glow somehow made me feel better. But I was too tired to go on. Sliding down the high, steep embankment, I dropped wearily to the ground.

I had barely fallen asleep when I was awakened by a thousand little pinpricks which set my arms, hands, and legs afire. Leaping up, I frantically brushed off my tormenters. My bed was on a nest of ants!

Scrambling back to the tracks I continued on my way. My arms and legs were swollen and hot. I had nothing to drink for hours, and my mouth seemed stuffed with cotton. When I rounded the long curve and saw the small station house, my body straightened, my pace lengthened.

The station was dark save for a single kerosene lamp in the dingy waiting room. I rapped on the closed door. After several knocks, each a little heavier than the one before, an old woman showed herself, peering suspiciously into my face. When I made the universal gesture of drinking, she nodded, handed me a metal dipper and pointed to a covered barrel next to the door. The water tasted stale, but it was cool and wet, and I reveled in dipper after dipper. Pumped full at last, I returned the dipper. Nodding my thanks, I lay down on the only bench in the waiting room, there to spend the remainder of the night in half-slumber, shivering and vaguely aware of the bedbugs that swarmed over me, further inflaming my skin.

But the sleep did its job and with the dawn I was on my way. I had not gone a mile when I spotted three Japanese gendarmes following me. Evidently they were notified by the station keeper. Alarmed, I ran, but in my weakened condition I was no match for my pursuers who caught up with me in a few minutes.

At the police station in the nearby village, consternation ran high. No one seemed to have any idea of what to do with me. Especially after I managed to somehow explain that I had no money and that I was on my way to Dairen. While the officials discussed my fate, at times quite heatedly, I took advantage of the situation long enough to walk out to a small market. There were a few coppers in my pocket. With these I bought three radishes. Then I strolled back to the station, where I had not even been missed. As I sat on a bench munching my radishes, someone brought me four rice dumplings and a cup of hot tea. I accepted gratefully and, fortified with the warm food, faced the future quite cheerfully. Surely the authorities, in order to rid themselves of the foreigner, would ship me at once to Dairen on the State Railroad. Shortly before noon, a constable took me to the depot. My heart sank the instant I saw the train. It was facing the wrong way. I remonstrated, mildly at first, then frantically, but my captor frowned and pushed me aboard. By late afternoon I was back in Mukden. Mukden and Dairen are equidistant. It would have been equally simple to send me to

Dairen. It was my first lesson in bureaucracy. The minds of bureaucrats do not function like those of normal people. At the Mukden station the constable pointed to the street and gave me a little shove. I somehow found the German Consulate, and after another good scolding, a meal, and enough money for a ticket, I was once more on my way.

In Dairen, I dutifully reported to the consul who arranged lodging for me. First, however, came the by-now-well-known sermon. The steamer *Duisburg* would arrive in three days and I was to board her as a second class passenger. My father, although he did not know it at the time, would pay the bill.

The day the ship arrived, I was sick. By 10 a.m. I was put to bed. An hour later, a hastily summoned Japanese doctor said I had smallpox. At noon, two other physicians, one the *Duisburg's* doctor, arrived and diagnosed it as pneumonia. By 2 p.m. I was in the hospital, and before dark I was in a coma, which lasted five days. It was an additional two days before I could understand what had happened. In addition to being close to death with pneumonia, I had a spinal infection, and a tracheal infection. To add to my misery, my body was covered with huge boils. A Japanese woman nurse watched over me day and night, sleeping on a mat on the floor beside my bed in order to be near.

But even as my body slowly fought the infections, a new, even worse, enemy began to infiltrate my being, threatening my sanity. It began the day I came out of the coma. I was awake for a short time, then fell asleep again, and instantly had a terrifying nightmare. In it, I was flying from the hospital window into a dark, stormy sky. Below me, the landscape was desolate and blighted. Abruptly I halted, hovering over the maw of a cold furnace. Then, to my horror, I began to fall, faster and faster, until utter blackness enveloped me, the blackness of oblivion. Each time I fell asleep the same dream recurred. The nightmare happened so regularly and seemed so real, that panic overcame me whenever I felt my eyes grow heavy with weariness, as I tried desperately to put off falling asleep. When the vice consul visited me after a particularly harrowing version of this dream, I told him firmly that I would absolutely refuse to leave the hospital via the window, and would walk, not fly to the hotel. He patted my hand and murmured, "Of course. Of course."

After a week of torment, and fearing for my sanity, I insisted on leaving, although I had not recovered. The doctor remonstrated, as did the consul, but I made such a fuss that they gave in. I dressed slowly, puffing and pausing often. Then, taking a deep breath, with a final fearful glance at the open window, I headed for the door. Once in the corridor I almost collapsed, but on the sidewalk I felt a little better and less giddy. My course resembled that of a drunk, as I staggered from curb to buildings and back, wending my way toward the hotel.

Recovery was very slow, and when the steamer *Leverkusen* docked, a few days later, I was glad to embark, even if it meant trouble at the end of the voyage. A day out of Dairen, my misery was further intensified by an infection which paralyzed my jaw muscles, preventing my mouth from closing. Thus I lay, feverish, my mouth agape, as the ship steamed southward to Yokohama, Nagasaki and Shanghai.

At Shanghai I felt the first faint stirrings of returning health. My jaw muscles relaxed, my appetite improved, my knees no longer shook. With the coming of tropical warmth, as we crossed the Tropic of Cancer, my strength came bounding back. In step with my ever-increasing feeling of well-being and the sight of flying fish and cavorting porpoises, my spirits climbed.

As my health improved the specter of what awaited me when the vessel arrived in Germany grew. The prospect of a prison term for jumping ship loomed blackly in the future. At Hong Kong I made up my mind and when the gangway was lowered to Manila's Pier Seven, I smiled at the Fourth Officer and stepped ashore. I had no money, no spare clothes. My passport was locked in the purser's safe to ensure that I could not go ashore in any foreign port. But it was a balmy day in May; the air, once I left the port area behind, was fragrant and clean. I was healthy once again and ready for any adventure. I had no idea where my next meal would come from, in this strange land ten thousand miles from home. But even as the thought came, I pushed it away, determined that nothing should dampen my soaring spirit.

But I could do nothing about the sudden deluge that came out of a seemingly cloudless sky and literally soaked me to the skin in a matter of seconds. Waterlogged and bedraggled, I ran into a nearby gas station and stood there, shivering and dripping while a puddle of water quickly formed at my feet. The rain stopped as abruptly as it had started. As I stepped into the sunshine to dry out, a Model T Ford chugged into the driveway and came to a coughing halt at the door of the station. A couple alighted. He was short, dark, and rather thin. She was doll-like, pretty and a bit on the plump side. After a curious glance at me, they entered the station, and almost immediately the woman stepped to the window and looked me over. The man, meanwhile, spoke to the young attendant, pointing my way occasionally. I was beginning to feel uncomfortable under the woman's persistent, though by no means hostile, scrutiny, and was moving away, when the man and woman emerged calling to me. He tried English, then Spanish, and finally, quite logically, Tagalog, the native language. I understood almost nothing of the first, and nothing at all of the others, so I could only shrug, and look dumb. On inspiration, I addressed him in German, but now it was his turn to shrug and look perplexed. The woman broke the stalemate by pointing at the Ford, and in another minute we were on our way.

We stopped, fifteen minutes later, in front of a two-story house in the old part of the city. The house was typically Spanish, with thick adobe walls, small barred windows on the ground floor and wide, unbarred ones above. The courtyard was long and a bit dark, but the moment the heavy front door was shut, the silence and coolness were a balm to both body and spirit. The upstairs was also typically Spanish, consisting of several bedrooms, an elaborate, high-ceilinged drawing room, a less-gorgeous dining room, a nondescript kitchen, and a less-than adequate bathroom. The house, I learned within the hour, belonged to Señor and Señora Caro, Juan and Carmen, a charming couple of Spanish-Filipino descent.

Moving in with the Caros brought me to the end of another phase of my life, a short one to be sure, but a dark one, a time of sickness, filled with terror of the unknown and the fear of oblivion. The future, whatever it held, surely would be for the better.

9

A Year In Manila

I remained with the kindly Caros for more than a year. Treated as a member of the family, I helped in an automobile repair shop and at the gasoline station, both of which they owned. It was a year in which I luxuriated in my new freedom, in the balmy tropical nights, in the easy, languid days. I buried my nose in books and magazines, mostly movie magazines. Without a teacher or dictionary it was difficult. Slowly, uncomprehendingly at first, then faster, more easily, I acquired a knowledge of the English language by sheer perseverance, often being frustrated by the simplest words such as: but, or, nor, husband, once. I took nightly walks, reveling in the warm, fragrant darkness, the glittering sky, the bright moon. I even reveled in the fury of the typhoons, the roaring deluges, the hot days and sticky nights. Only the meals caused me some measure of discomfort at first. It wasn't the quality that bothered me, but the time at which they were served. Being used to strict shipboard scheduling, it was more than a little disconcerting to have breakfast at nine, lunch at two, a *merienda* at five, and dinner at half past nine or even ten p.m.

For the first time in my life I went to church. Tall, stately, Belgian-built San Sebastian church was a magnificent building. I admired the atmosphere within the big cathedral, the furnishings, the lofty cross, but I understood not a word of the mass. I had, in fact, never before even heard the Latin tongue. But I kneeled, folded my hands, mumbled the chants, looked, or hoped I looked, pious, and thus managed to remain inconspicuous. I went out of respect for my "family," not because of desire on my part. Secretly I was sure there was no use in going, for there was no God.

I had my first misgivings about the Catholic religion after Midnight Mass on Christmas Eve. Drinking began in the houses around us. Risqué anecdotes, unseemly jests and even curses came to the fore. I wondered how a man could piously genuflect before Christ and then, a bare hour later, use the same Christ's name as a curse word in drunken babble. And as I walked along the noisy streets, I couldn't help comparing the raucous atmosphere with the profound stillness of my native land on the evening before Christmas. There the bars closed their doors at six o'clock, streetcars ran only infrequently, no harsh tunes were permitted and only soft Christmas songs broke the silence of the night. Silent Night, Holy Night was just that. Even my atheist father had sung the familiar carols, so infectious was the Christmas spirit in Germany.

New Year was welcomed boisterously with firecrackers, horns and confetti. Downtown Manila was crowded and unbelievably noisy and gay. Once again, after the Mass, drunkenness and hangovers prevailed in the brightly lighted and adorned houses. While I had some grave doubts about the Catholic religion, I had none at all about the merrymaking. I joined in with youthful zest and exuberance.

Early in the year, a little daughter joined the Caro household and was duly named Vilma, after the reigning actress of the day.

Another summer passed, another season of typhoons and deluges, and yet another chapter of my life was about to close. Nothing marred the pages as day followed unhurried, eventless day. My English improved markedly to the point that I was able to read a complete book, missing no more than a third of it.

10

The Gospel Ship

A person seldom knows until afterward when life takes a new tack. But this time I knew exactly. It was on the ninth of September, 1932, at sunset that a new chapter of my life opened. Across the street from the gas station the musicians on the long, narrow, palm-lined dance floor of the Legaspi Landing Cabaret were tuning their instruments. In the harbor, elements of the U.S. Asiatic Fleet lay at anchor. A boat disembarked Shore Patrolmen on the floating dock behind the cabaret, followed quickly by several boatloads of white-uniformed sailors. To my right, the sun was setting behind Bataan Peninsula. Dusk was falling and with it came a welcome coolness. In the swiftly-gathering darkness I saw a white yacht approach her anchorage a bare hundred yards from the Manila Hotel. As my eyes caressed her slender hull, the tall, raked masts and yellow funnel, she came to a stop.

The Gospel Ship Fukuin Maru *or "Good Tidings," which was to be my home far longer than I anticipated. From the author's collection.*

Her anchor splashed into the slightly-choppy water. The anchor light quickly soared aloft. She swung into the wind and lay still, white water bubbling around her.

A vague excitement rippled through me for reasons I couldn't understand. I had never seen that particular ship before. Throughout the night as I watched the station, I glanced frequently at the motionless yacht, trying to fathom the quiver of anticipation within me. I felt drawn to the vessel, even as the heavy fragrance from the nearby flower beds mingled with the subdued tunes of the orchestra on the cabaret's lantern-lit dance floor and wafted seaward. Somehow I knew the gentle offshore breeze carried my future with it.

Before noon the next day, a ship chandler gave me a ride in his launch, and presently I stood on the yacht's teakwood main deck. The ship had weathered a typhoon on the way from Japan, and there was some damage on the deck. The captain, a somewhat heavy, ruddy faced man of about fifty, with blue-gray eyes, a double chin, and close cut gray hair, stood nearby. I told myself I was there out of mere curiosity, but suddenly a desire to roam the seas once again welled within me. The captain asked if I knew anything about diesel engines. Just that. I answered with a simple, "No." He nodded and said, "Good. You'll be assistant engineer." Both the captain, whose name was Skolfield, and the chief engineer, a lanky Swede named Nordstrom, assured me that knowledge of the workings of a diesel engine was not required, only the willingness to learn. The pay was commensurate with my expertise, but I cared little about that. I was delighted to be on a ship once more. I said goodbye to the kindly Caros and was off.

During the two weeks we lay at anchor, it never occurred to me to inquire about our itinerary. There was enough to do to keep my mind on other things. The ship came from Japan and ran into a typhoon off the north coast of Luzon. The littered engine room needed cleaning. Repairs to the engine were required. Stores, fuel and water must be taken on.

The yacht was 130 feet long, with a 24-foot beam and powered by a Swedish diesel engine. She was registered in Boston under the name of *Fukuin Maru* and flew the Stars and Stripes. She was built of wood but copper-sheathed below the waterline. In addition to the engine, she was schooner rigged. Her sails could make use of the wind, if necessary. The crew's quarters were forward, the officers' amidships, and the skipper's office and staterooms aft. In addition there was a large, unoccupied stateroom just abaft the engine room. The crew consisted of sixteen men of seven nationalities: Captain, American; Doctor, American; Chief Officer, Norwegian; Chief Engineer, Swedish, Second Officer, Filipino; Assistant Engineer, German; Captain's Boy, Japanese; Cook, Chinese; Dentist, Nurse and Sailors, Filipinos.

The Islands of the Sulu Sea

We sailed shortly before noon on a bright day in late September. The sunlight sparkled on the lively water; a fresh southwesterly breeze was blowing, raising an occasional whitecap. It was a day when it felt good to be alive and at sea. We were passing the island of Corregidor, at the mouth of Manila Bay, when I finally asked where we were going, what sort of ship I was on, and how long we would be gone. Incredibly, the answers to the first two queries were helpless shrugs. Neither the mate nor the engineer knew, except that the ship was cleared for "southern ports." To question number three the chief engineer replied that he guessed it would be about a week. A week! In reality, the planet would make a complete circuit about the sun before we entered Manila Bay again, a year and two weeks later!

My first inkling of the sort of activities the ship was engaged in came the morning after departure. We were on a south-south-westerly course all night and were approaching the island of Busuanga, north of the long barrier island of Palawan. At 8 o'clock all off-watch hands were ordered on deck. I was in the engine room, but by looking at the open skylight from an angle, I could see mirrored in its glass the reflection of the deck area around the mainmast. Captain Skolfield stood there, a book in his hand. It was a black-covered book. The seaman's articles? When the crew had gathered, the skipper began to read. I watched idly, pleased with my spy mirror. I heard nothing save the thunder of the engine, but I could tell when he raised his voice, for now and then he would look up from the book and address the men. His mouth opened wider and he seemed to become more intense. I made a round of the engine room checking oil pressure, temperatures, vibrations, as I was taught. Then I returned to my observation post, and my mouth dropped open, which was not hard because I was looking straight upward. The captain's head was bowed. In front of him, a few of the crew were looking around, but for the most part they stood or sat quietly, with bowed heads. A terrible realization struck me. The skipper was praying. Praying! But why? And that book. I had seen a Bible once. It, too, was black. I tried to dismiss the disquieting thoughts. So, the "old man" read the Bible. Many men of the sea did that. But why call the crew together? More than a little upset, I met the chief engineer at the door as he came to check on me a few minutes later. He took me to his cabin which adjoined the engine room. I did not understand all he told me, for neither of us spoke perfect English, but I caught enough to wish I had never seen the yacht. When he finished I knew four things: the ship belonged to a Baptist Mission; our objective would be to investigate the ethnic backgrounds of the various tribes which lived on the remote southern islands; we would go as far south as — and that was when my heart skipped several beats — Borneo, and be gone for a year; and fourth, we all would be required to attend daily devotions. I had no idea what devotions of any kind were, let alone daily ones.

Thinking about it later, I couldn't help smiling at the ironic twist of fate which deposited me, after all that wandering, into the one situation I would have most carefully avoided had I known it was coming. What, I wondered, would my father say when he found out? In a letter, not a month before, he informed me that he always knew where I was, even if I didn't bother to write, by the names of the countries on the bills that came for the "assistance" I periodically received. The unexpected expense was quite upsetting to him. Dealing him the ultimate blow by joining the "enemy," I was rather glad to be out of his reach. A stern Prussian, he made it abundantly clear throughout my youth that any mention of religion would not be regarded kindly. He even went so far as to request that the school authorities excuse me from the weekly religious instruction and put me in a science class instead. And now, this. Sighing resignedly, I turned my thoughts to more pleasant things.

My mother and father's wedding picture shows him at his Prussian best. From the author's collection.

My watch over, I lunched and went on deck. We were running parallel to a beach of dazzling white sand rimmed with tall, slender, curving palms. As always when viewing new sights, my heartbeat increased. The beach, the blue water lapping at it, the green palm trees, the hazy mountain behind, the white, cottony clouds sailing in the dark-blue sky, were exactly as I had so often visualized. I strained my eyes for a glimpse of coconuts on the trees, but at that distance saw none. It mattered little, for within a day, I knew, I expected to be standing beneath these stately trees. A village came into view, its presence announced by the blue-gray haze of cooking fires. A large number of boats, their thin masts pointing like fingers at the sky, were beached nearby above the highwater mark. It required keen eyes to see the small brown huts among the trees, but my eyes were sharp and I spotted one almost immediately. After negotiating a long, narrow, winding channel that taxed the skipper's skill, we anchored a scant hundred yards off the town of Coron.

11

Palawan

The following day was a Sunday, and I attended my first service in a Baptist Church. I didn't go out of any desire for spiritual food but because of the opportunity it afforded me to see the town. The church was small, a mere shack with a few crude pews on the dirt floor and a relatively ornate pulpit with a long, yellow cross on the front. Behind the pulpit, on the bamboo-mat wall hung a plaque with the words "Jesus Saves" in raised letters.

The service itself remains a blank in my memory. I was interested in other things. While the skipper preached and the local pastor interpreted, my eyes made the rounds of the little room. It was all so new and wonderfully strange; the coarsely-dressed barefoot men, the small black-eyed, black-haired, barefoot women, the almost naked children, the lizards on the walls, the coconut trees outside the windows.

The service was over before I had time to get bored. After a lamely sung hymn and a long closing prayer, neither of which I understood, I found myself shaking limp hands. Taught that a firm handshake was the mark of a man, I didn't know what to think. The lifeless hands were disconcerting and somehow disappointing. It was years before I learned that the hearty, knuckle-cracking handshake of the West is not for the people of the East. There one shakes hands gently and delicately with only the merest suggestion of pressure.

We sailed after lunch, avoiding the tortuous entrance channel, heading southwest instead. Our course took us past the rocky ramparts of Coron Island toward the leper colony of Culion on the island of the same name. I had never seen a leper, let alone an entire colony of the untouchables. It was with a great deal of interest that I stood at the port rail as we ran up the deep inlet. Although we passed close by the colony, I saw nothing strange. A rather neat village of thatched houses, a long, iron-roofed building, which seemed to be a shop or small factory, children playing, women with baskets on their heads striding purposefully along, a group of men launching a boat. Only when we moored to the single pier did I see the fence and gate, the closed gate, which separated the healthy from the sick.

An hour after our arrival an elderly, white-haired white man came aboard and was ushered to the captain's quarters. He left a half hour later, after a quick tour of the ship. That night, the skipper, the doctor, and I — the chief mate and the chief engineer declined — dined at the man's bungalow, high on the hill. The Reverend Mr. and Mrs. Jansen were missionaries and had been working in the colony for twenty years. As we sat on the narrow veranda, enjoying the coolness of the night and the fragrance that rose from the garden below us, I learned something about leprosy. It was comforting information. Leprosy, Mr. Jansen assured us, was not nearly as contagious as was generally believed. In fact it was rather difficult to contract. Only basic precautions were needed to protect oneself. The disease, he said, was transmitted only through open wounds or cracks in the skin. Both he and his wife had handled lepers for many years, yet had remained untouched by the loathsome affliction. Thus, a simple touch or a handshake could not possibly transmit leprosy unless the bacillus had access to the bloodstream. Lysol-filled basins, he assured us, were placed throughout the colony for the protection of visitors. Only the year before, the authorities had issued a decree permitting lepers to marry. At once, Mrs. Jansen said, the atmosphere in the colony changed, becoming brighter, more cheerful, as life suddenly had meaning again. Gone was the unutterable melancholy, the loneliness, the despair. But one source of sorrow remained, and would always exist: the offspring of leprous parents, uncontaminated themselves, were removed at birth. Aside from this and, of course, the nature of the disease itself, the inhabitants of the colony lived a fairly normal life.

A few hours on a southwesterly course brought us to Bacuit, a relatively large town on the northern tip of Palawan. Our evangelist's endeavors began there, running afoul of the Roman Church almost at once. On the second day I accompanied the team, consisting of the doctor, the dentist, a nurse and two evangelists headed by the skipper. The moment we landed we were joined by natives. First little children appeared, then older ones, and finally their elders, who tagged along until we came to a halt not far from the massive Roman Church. The captain, through an interpreter for the benefit of those who could not understand English, invited the people to avail themselves of our medical services. After a few minutes, a woman pushed a little boy toward the doctor and explained, somewhat bashfully, that the youngster had worms. The ice broken, others stepped forward — worms, toothaches, malaria, tropical ulcers, infections. Some were treated on the spot, others were requested to come to the ship.

The doctoring done, the skipper held up his hands to quiet the chatter and began to preach. Again, I remember nothing of the sermon, being too enchanted with the surroundings. Suddenly the church bells began to peal. At first softly, then louder and louder until the town fairly shook with the mighty sound of bells.

Now the ringing of bells in a Roman Church is strictly regulated. One can readily imagine the consternation among the faithful when they heard the pealing of the heavy bells when they weren't supposed to peal. At the outset, the skipper tried to overcome the din by raising his voice, but no human throat can compete with three one-ton bells two

hundred yards away. He soon gave up and, circulating among the onlookers, invited them to visit the ship, where the bells couldn't follow. The priest was doubtlessly watching from the belfry, for the instant we walked away, the clanging stopped. Drowsy silence fell once more.

Thereafter, in the vicinity of a Roman Church, the team had two choices: conduct the meetings as far away from the offending bells as possible, or, if this was not feasible, speak quickly and crowd as much as possible into the message. In the latter event, the speaker brought his message to an end, knowing he had only a few moments of silence left. In this way the message could be delivered before the priest became aware of "the enemy" and located the bellringer who, more often than not, was among the rapt listeners.

The priest's conduct elicited caustic comments even from staunch Catholics. More important, it proved conclusively, according to the skipper after a particularly loud and vicious ringing, that the priests, propagators of fear, were determined that their flock should never be exposed to the light of pure Bible teaching. He firmly believed that ignorance and darkness were the chains wherewith the church of Rome kept millions of unfortunates around the world in fetters. I cared not either way, but I thought the action of the priests quite unsporting, nevertheless.

Skirting the western coast of Palawan, we felt the full force of a heavy quartering sea. The yacht rolled alarmingly, often submerging her rails, although they were seven feet above the water. On deck, even the shortest walk became hazardous. On the slippery engine room plates, a single step could be disastrous. My watch over, I went to the bridge and looked around. The day was coming to an end. To the left, already wrapped in a blue haze, ranged the Palawan mountains. On the right, the sun touched the rim of the world, turning the whitecaps into bloody froth. The sea was empty, empty and lonely for a thousand miles from the white beaches of Palawan to the littered strands of Indo-China. Stepping into the wheelhouse, I looked at the chart. The names fairly leaped off the paper: Cape Ross, Enterprise Point, Emergency Point, Wedge Island, Middle Shoal, York Breakers and, reaching farther into the China Sea, Temple Bank, Seahorse Shoal, Fairy Queen, Lord Auckland Shoal. Ah, the romance of it, I thought, enthralled by the tiny names on the yellow-white paper. And I was a part of it, a part of the Age of Discovery. The tail end, to be sure, but a part, nonetheless, for I, too, would walk where few or no white men had ever walked and see sights never beheld by Western eyes.

We slipped into the quiet water of Malampaya Sound as the last glimmer of light went, anchoring not far from the few yellow lamps of a village. Once the engine stopped, the silence was overwhelming. At nine o'clock, when the generator was shut down and electricity switched over to batteries, the stillness was almost absolute. I stayed on deck long after the dim lights ashore went out, bewitched by the beautiful night, the glittering stars, the unearthly quiet, the heady fragrance of night flowers which, although there was no wind, wafted across the narrow strip of water and enveloped the ship like a scented veil. Thus the hours slipped by, silently, serenely, gloriously. Occasionally, a fish broke the surface with a silvery slap, or the sleepy bark of a dog rang through the night, and once I heard the harsh cry of a night bird. But the sound, far from marring the peace, only emphasized it. At last, weary, and a bit chilled, I turned in.

12

Crocodile Sound

We remained in the bay for a week, during which I received a foretaste of the life in the coming months. It was a life that, like the tropics, was geared to the sun, ambling on, slowly, lazily, uneventfully. The contrast to the hectic, nervous, anxiety-filled existence I knew in my own country was stark. Day began at six-thirty, or seven, or seven-thirty, or even eight o'clock if one chose to skip breakfast. But the best time was before seven, when the coolness of the night still lingered, before the dew dried on the teakwood rails and the vendors swarmed around the ship. Invariably, between seven and eight, a cry rang across the still water as peddlers boarded the ship. "Fish for sale. Fresh fish for sale." Just as predictably, Ah Chong, the cook, stepped from his small galley, gave the fish a disinterested look, and named an absurdly low sum. This brought instant jeers from the vendors. Thereafter, the haggling, so dear to the Oriental soul, consumed another fifteen minutes. When words failed, as was often the case in a country of many dialects, gestures sufficed: a raised eyebrow, a vigorous shake of the head, three lifted fingers that grew hesitantly to four, to five, a final nod and a grin. Then came the sellers of mangoes and bananas, of coconuts and melons, of cashew fruits and cashew nuts, of papayas and tamarind, of eggs and meats. Promptly at eight o'clock the skipper, Bible in hand, appeared on deck and for fifteen minutes the only sound on board was the skipper's voice as first he read, then explained the Biblical passages.

Only twice during the first two weeks had my interest been awakened in what the skipper said, and then only temporarily. Each scripture text took me back to early childhood. Above the sofa in our living room hung a large tapestry, artfully embroidered in gold on purple with the words, "*Sei getreu bis in den tod, und ich will dir die krone des lebens geben.*" It had a nice ring to it and was easily memorized. A poem, my father said, just a poem. The meaning? He shrugged and turned away. That quiet, sunny morning I had the answer, ten thousand miles from our living room, in another language. I listened attentively and wondered why my father tolerated the tapestry at all. The skipper closed the book, gazed at the sparkling water and, as if to himself, repeated the verse, "Be thou faithful unto death, and I will give thee a crown of life."

The other verse referred to the rich man and the beggar Lazarus. Somehow, the story crept into a class discussion when I was in the fourth grade. My teacher, a young woman of nobility, with some vehemence, accused God of casting the rich man into hell because he refused to feed the beggar. She exhorted us never to forget the story of this vengeful God. I didn't forget. In fact I often pondered the illogic of it for there was no God at all. How could someone who doesn't exist cast a rich man into hell? That morning in early October I heard the account again, but coming from the skipper, it sounded different. In the absence of my father's strong will, the story became credible. The rich man, the captain emphasized, was cast into the fire not because he refused to help the beggar, but (although it was merely by implication) for his rejection of God. That sounded reasonable *if* the account were true and *if* there really were a God.

Thus far, the captain always made the closing prayer. That morning he looked at the chief engineer. Would he pray? The Swede shook his head. The chief officer, sensing that he would be next, quickly held out both hands, palms forward. At that instant I decided to count the coconut trees bordering the nearby beach.

"Kurt?"

I stopped counting and looked at the skipper.

"Will you pray?"

I had never said a prayer and could not have concocted one, so I, too, shook my head, a bit sheepishly.

Devotions over, we, or most of us, heaved a collective sigh of relief and went to work. There was little to do; polish the brass on the engine or on the skylight, paint a little, replenish the battery water. On deck it was no different; wash down, varnish a door here, a window there, paint a little, chip a little, polish the compass, the telegraph, splice a rope, mend a tarpaulin. By noon, or often before, the work was done. After lunch, a long siesta, a short swim in the water, then perhaps an excursion ashore.

I say a short swim, for Malampaya Sound had another, more apt name: Crocodile Sound. We always swam together, thrashing wildly and creating as great a disturbance as possible. It was thought this would scare the creatures away. We also kept a wary eye on the bridge where a lookout kept watch for the tell-tale V-shaped ripple. It never occurred to us that a hungry saurian might approach his dinner beneath the surface, or that our thrashing might attract him.

The Islands of the Sulu Sea

At supper one evening, the chief officer casually remarked on how my white skin gleamed in the water, in contrast to those of my brown-skinned shipmates. Which, he wondered aloud, would a crocodile or a shark spot first? I immediately started a regimen of prolonged sunbaths.

My first close-up of the huge reptiles came the following day. In the company of a sailor and the cabin boy I made a short trip up a small river. The water was muddy, probably due to one of the brief but fierce tropical showers farther inland. It was dark on the river despite the glaring sun. The trees on both banks reached across and joined branches, forming a dark-green canopy. Spotting an edible species of shellfish on the gnarled, gaunt mangroves at the water's edge, the boy steered the boat toward the nearer bank. We tied the craft to a root and, knee-deep in the water, proceeded to collect the clams. As I turned to throw a handful into the boat, I froze, my hands suspended over the gunwale. I was staring directly into three pairs of baleful eyes not twenty feet away. Only the eyes and the tips of the pointed snouts were visible. Three crocodiles! One for each of us or, rather, as flashed through my mind, one of us for each of them. I

dropped the clams into the boat; then, in a foolish effort to frighten them, waded toward the reptiles.

"Don't!" The sailor's voice was sharp. "As long as we can see them, we're all right."

It was too late. At my third step, the crocodiles sank silently and with scarcely a ripple. I stopped, suddenly terrified, straining to pierce the muddy water with wide-open eyes, expecting at any moment to feel the crunch of their foul jaws on my legs.

"Come on!" the sailor cried.

Abruptly my befuddled mind cleared and I flung myself head first into the boat. We cast off and rowed away. Looking back, I saw three pairs of disappointed eyes intently follow us.

Back aboard ship, we retraced our course, rounding the tip of Palawan. A day's run across the Cuyo passage brought us to the Cuyo Islands, in the northern section of the Sulu Sea. I fell in love with the main island of Cuyo the instant I saw it. The coconut palms grew thick and tall; the beach of white sand ran in a great, sweeping arc the length of the town, bisected only by a short stone pier. The streets were relatively wide, the stilt houses tidy. Each had its own bamboo fence and leather-hinged gate. There was a massive Roman Church, an adequate school, a small post office with spindly telegraph tower, four stores, and a restaurant of sorts. The only motorized transportation was an old truck that brought the produce of the outlying villages to the town. A small inter-island steamer called bi-monthly, anchoring just off the pier. But if the island and its vicinity was charming during the daylight hours, the nights were utterly alluring. When the last pearly glimmer of the zodiacal light died, high up, the planet earth as I knew it from childhood ceased to be. As the darkness swiftly deepened and stars sprang forth, the purple vault above seemed to expand and draw away, making room for yet more suns until the searching eye found not the smallest void. No mortal can describe so awesome a grandeur; it must be experienced, its tranquility felt, its music heard. And when, toward midnight, a faint offshore breeze, gentle and soft as the breath of a sleeping child, sprang up, blowing the perfume of a million flowers over the warm water, I could only gasp with wonder, awed, and a little afraid of such unearthly splendor.

The Islands of the Sulu Sea

Cuyo became our southern headquarters to which we returned periodically for mail, oil, and stores deposited there for us. It was at Cuyo that I had my closest brush with death one shining afternoon, a brush that left an indelible mark. It was a sport among us to dive under the hull amidships and surface on the opposite side, a dive of twelve feet down, thirty feet across and twelve feet up. No great feat, admittedly, requiring merely strong limbs and some lung capacity. We thought little of it until that bright afternoon when I, alone in the water at the time, took a deep breath and headed downward. The sea was calm; the ship rose and fell almost imperceptibly on a long gentle swell. I leisurely inspected the bottom as I swam downward. Approaching the keel, I noticed a slight swirl of sand. I should have recognized the warning, but didn't. The instant I realized my peril, it was too late. The back of my head touched the keel even as my face plowed a furrow into the sand. Pushing frantically, I freed my face, but my shoulders were caught. The pressure on my back increased noticeably, and in a flash I realized what was happening. We were anchored in shallow water, with a mere fathom or less under the keel at high tide. Now the tide was low, the ship almost aground. The lazy swell lifted and lowered the ship in a slow rhythm. Close to panic, I tried desperately digging a channel even as I felt the barnacles dig into my flesh. In vain. As fast as I scooped the sand, it ran back. My lungs began to ache. I tried expanding my chest, but it wouldn't flex. Eventually, I knew the ship would lift, but would I then lie, crushed, on the ocean floor? I felt the vibration of the generator through the keel. A scant ten feet above me people were sitting in the sunlight, breathing the sweet, clear air. To ease the almost unbearable weight I exhaled the air in my lungs. A great bubble rose past my face toward the surface. My head swam; a piercing whistle attacked my eardrums; my vision blurred; the blue water turned gray and darkened. At last the pressure abated as the ship slowly, agonizingly slowly, rose. I pushed myself clear, oblivious of the raking barnacles, and drifted upward along the hulk, further lacerating my body on the razor-sharp shells. How delicious the air tasted, how lovely the blue sky looked, how golden the sun. How wonderful it was to be alive. In later years my work occasionally demanded that I inspect missile systems on submarines. Each time I entered their cramped spaces the dreaded feeling returned.

Christmas found us still at anchor off Cuyo. Three months had elapsed since I joined the yacht, three months of pure joy on the tropical seas. I was alone on the beach that 24th of December, watching the sun, a huge ball of burnished copper, sink slowly into the sea. Idly I sat on the warm sand, letting the white grains run through my fingers, my thoughts following the sun's travel across the world. In each land the fiery giver of life would be a bit higher in the sky -- Siam, India, Persia, Turkey, Germany. Germany! Without warning a wave of homesickness rolled over me, leaving me gasping. I stared at the red sun, fighting to restrain the tears. It would be noon in my country, or a little before. Noon on Christmas Eve, the most pleasant day of the year. Already, the rooms where stood the Christmas trees were heavy with the fragrance of pine, apple, marzipan, gingerbread. The goose, stuffed, and plump, was sitting on the kitchen table, ready for the oven. Abruptly, as I sat, alone, on a deserted beach on an island in the middle of the Sulu Sea, far from home, the tears fell, a hot flood gushing from the deep well of utter loneliness, a wracking, wrenching yet strangely healing, soothing stream which flowed freely until the well was dry. I sat for a long time, while the last light of day died in the west and the profound silence of the tropic night descended, subtly imparting its peace and serenity to my soul. Then I drew a somewhat tremulous breath, plunged into the warm phosphorescent water, and swam for the ship.

13

Tropical Medicine

We sailed the day after Christmas, recrossing the Sulu Sea to the island of Palawan. Once again, as the ship met the gentle swells, I pored over the chart spread on the wheelhouse table, murmuring the strange names — Queen of the Sea Shoal, Tubbataha Reef, Sultana Shoal, Charybdis Shoal, and a large mysterious patch encircled with a dotted line: Unsurveyed Area.

It was at Palawan that our exploration, missionary and medical work began in earnest. The following weeks brought a bewildering series of villages, little and large, with tongue-twisting names, lying either along the shore or sometimes hidden in lush valleys or straggling up the sides of mountains. Our ship created quite a stir for few or no white men had ever seen them before. There was no cove where our anchors did not splash into the still water, no promontory which did not echo the dull booming of our diesel, no lagoon whose crystal waters were not stirred by our propeller. As day followed seemingly endless day, while the sun ambled across the dark-blue sky and the moon drifted over the heavenly arch, life moved like a slow-motion film. The bays and coves, too, never varied, topazes set in emeralds by day, mysterious purple pearls by night. Only life on board changed, becoming slower and lazier as the days stretched into weeks, the weeks into months.

In February, the middle of the dry season, our potable water supply became critically low and the tanks were padlocked. We never went thirsty, but water for bathing and washing was rationed — a quarter bucket daily for the deckhands, a third for the engineers. Halved bamboo tubes were rigged along the lower edges of the awnings which covered the decks. Then, at the slightest sign of rain, the crew was alerted. It mattered little if the time was noon or midnight or break of day. When the call, "all hands on deck" came, we jumped, captain, doctor, cook, <u>all</u> hands. For five minutes the rain was allowed to wash the awnings clean before diverting it to fill the tanks. Only then were we permitted to bathe and wash. In a moment, shorts and shirts were off and sixteen bodies feverishly lathered, for we never knew how long a shower or a squall would last. Often this occurred at two or three in the morning. After the bath, the clothes were just as frantically scraped and rinsed. It felt wonderful to be clean once again, free of salt crystals on skin and scalp. It was gratifying, too, to see the tanks bubble over with soft, sparkling water.

I heard much preaching in those days and often found it interesting. Not in a spiritual sense, but in the same way that I found all new things interesting. For the first time in my eighteen years I learned the real reason for Christmas, for Gethsemane, for Easter, for Good Friday. For the first time I was acquainted with the details of the Creation, of Adam and Eve. For the first time I had a graphic glimpse of heaven and hell. Fascinating though they were, I put them into the same category as our German Nibelungen, with the legends of Wotan and Thor, and the Walkyries. I found the theory of evolution quite believable while classifying the Biblical account of the Creation as pure fantasy. But it was all quite interesting and I memorized scripture verses by the dozen. Here and there other men or women, less burdened with the ability to reason than I, bowed their head in prayer and submission. One by one my shipmates yielded their wills and souls to a Higher Power, while we three Europeans would have none of it. Occasionally, the skipper took me aside for a quiet chat about my soul, my sins, my ultimate destination. I was quite happy with the way life was unfolding before me, happy to be a free man in a country of cheerful, hospitable people, in a land where the days and nights were lovely beyond description. Yes, life was indeed beautiful. What more did I need? But I did not mention this during the sometimes long sessions. I listened respectfully, as became a youngster, agreed readily, then went on my way; my broad, pleasant, carefree way.

While living with the Caros in Manila, I discovered that Filipinos had certain virtues which, while not unknown to Westerners, are by no means popular practices among them. I refer to courtesy, hospitality, and filial piety. At first I felt highly uncomfortable, even a little embarrassed, to see grown, even elderly men, kiss the old ones upon entering or leaving the house. Eventually I found it quite pleasing. I learned, too, that one should never leave another person without first excusing himself, nor should one walk between people who were talking or looking at each other, without bowing as they passed. Children, even married ones, did not leave the house without first requesting permission, and they never argued with their elders. Yet although these goodly ways were practiced in the cities, they had a certain vagueness about them and were performed somewhat perfunctorily. It was in the country, among the simple and unaffected people that such manners really shined. One saw it in the eyes of the youngsters, as they kneeled and kissed the hands of the old ones and murmured an endearing name, and in the blessing they received in return in the form of a sometimes trembling hand laid gently on head or shoulder. One saw it in the manner in which even adults complied with their elders' not always reasonable wishes. There was nothing forced about the hospitality of the Filipino people, and their courtly, "Come, join us," should a stranger arrive at mealtime, is often welcome and always refreshing.

Only among the "heathen," which was how we termed the non-Christians, it seemed different. (It is an interesting fact that Christians, in turn, were often referred to as "infidels" by non-Christians.) Of course, the outer islands were different. Here, they were shy, these wild ones, shy and suspicious, and often hostile, as one is naturally suspicious and hostile toward the unknown, toward that which intrudes. And intrude we did, with our big ship, our noisy, gleaming engine, our electric lights. Intrude we did, even with our medicines and our sometimes boisterous good will, our ignorance of age-old customs and taboos. We found evidence enough of this perceived intrusion as we trudged along dusty paths, over mountain trails, through snake-infested jungles, in the deserted villages along the way. Many villages were empty save for a fearful man or woman too old or feeble to flee. Occasionally the villages were entirely empty but for a few snarling, yelping dogs. But if many were wary, many were also curious. Curious enough to venture from their jungle hideaways at the call of the interpreter and emerge with their yaws, their tropical ulcers, their gangrene, their boils. They came fearfully and timidly at first. Always cautious and watchful, they frequently bolted into the green maze at the first untoward movement. In time they became bolder.

Then came the day when the first *Tagbanua* stepped aboard the yacht. We watched him come, his paddle flashing slower and slower as he approached the ship. Warned by the skipper, we went about our tasks, pretending to ignore the lone figure in the small canoe. Twice he circumnavigated the yacht, then, encouraged by the interpreter's friendly shouts and wave, he came alongside the gangway, tied his craft with a loose knot and slowly ascended the steps. Refusing to step on the deck, he seated himself on the bulwark, one leg braced against it, the other on the top step of the gangway. His hands, fingers spread, pushed nervously against the broad rail. He was a handsome man, about five and a half feet tall, lean but not skinny. His jet-black hair reached almost to his shoulders; his face and body were hairless. He was naked save for a small loincloth. A small bag dangled against his left leg, a short machete against his right. He reminded me of Tarzan of the Apes, whose films I had seen in Manila, Tarzan when first encountered by white hunters. The *Tagbanua's* eyes were wide open and alert as he scanned the deck. Like a gazelle, he was poised for instant flight. One could sense the quiver in his slender limbs.

We stopped working and stared at the wild man. Abruptly, although no one had moved, he whirled, ran down the gangway, and furiously paddled away, leaving a series of violent eddies behind him.

An hour later, a small flotilla of outrigger canoes approached the ship. We watched apprehensively. Then we spied women and children and relaxed. A few moments later, they swarmed on the decks. Their scout had given us a clean "bill of health." Only mildly shy, they roamed the ship, staring at the shiny engine through the open skylight, rubbing rough, calloused hands over the bright fittings and glossy paint. Some pressed their ears against the engine room casing to hear the low humming of the generator.

One young stalwart stood motionless under an overhead light, which someone had turned on, staring fixedly at the bright filament. Taking a deep breath, he directed a stream of betel nut-scented air at the light. When it did not even flicker, he turned, jabbering excitedly in high-pitched staccato tones, pointing to the light. Instantly, he was surrounded by half a dozen of his fellow tribesmen, all gawking solemnly at the bulb.

Meanwhile, the doctor examined a few of the visitors and gave injections where indicated. At once those who had not received injections insisted that they, too, were entitled to the same treatment. The doctor bluntly refused. Medicines were expensive, and money was, and still is, a rare commodity in mission work. Worse, still, was the problem of replenishing the medical supply. So he frowned angrily and shook his head. At once the smiles disappeared from the faces of our visitors. Women and children were quickly shoved to one side of the ship. The men then spoke to the interpreter loudly, lengthily, with many a violent gesture, and much spitting of red betel nut juice. Swallowing, the interpreter turned to the doctor.

"More better you give them sir. They...they want it."

To my amazement, the doctor grinned, threw up his hands and shrugged. I followed him into the dispensary. Taking a bottle from a shelf he held it so I could read the label. It said, "Distilled water, sterile." He drew the clear liquid into a huge syringe, gravely swabbed each brown arm, and plunged the needle into the tough hides. The process was painful, as the grimaces plainly showed, but the moment the needle was withdrawn, the faces brightened and the decks rang with laughter. In a few minutes the tribespeople were gone, jabbering, giggling, and rubbing their sore arms. Like children, I thought, spoiled children. Gay, and full of mirth one moment, they could be petulant and hostile the next. That is not to say that those characteristics are confined to tribal natives, as anyone knows who has ever refused to lend money to a friend or, having lent it, endeavors to get it back.

14

Lost in the Jungle

As the months stretched into half a year, then to three quarters, both the chief officer and the chief engineer became restive. Mr. Farjoe, the mate and an old China hand, talked ceaselessly of the China Coast, the Yangtze, the Hong Kong-Canton run, and it became increasingly clear that his days aboard the yacht were numbered. The chief engineer, too, was longing for new fields, namely the rich gold mines of Bontoc or Paracale on the island of Luzon. I was happy enough, but the languid life was beginning to lose its appeal for me as well.

Then, with the onset of the south-west monsoon, fresh food became scarce. Our diet consisted mainly of corned beef, canned salmon or sardines, with only an occasional fresh fish or turtle. Morale fell rapidly.

The Islands of the Sulu Sea

We were excited one rainwashed morning to see the head of a wild boar moving through the placid water of the lagoon in which we were anchored. Hastily, for the lagoon was not wide, three sailors leaped into the boat. The brawniest, armed with an ax, manned the bow, the others took the oars. From the galley came the exuberant clatter of pots and pans. Soon we heard the steady swish-swish of knives being honed. Watching the boat eagerly, we could already savor the fresh, juicy meat. Then we saw the oarsmen abruptly rest their oars while the boar's head moved steadily away. We looked at each other. Our puzzlement turned to consternation when the boat suddenly veered and came back. Even before it had come within a quarter mile we had the answer, for sound carries easily in a quiet lagoon. It had not been a boar, after all, only the putrefied head of a boar being carried by a crocodile to its lair.

The skipper, as disappointed as we were, beckoned to me and led the way to his office. There he handed me a ten peso bill and told me to go ashore and get a cow. I nodded and was off. I had no idea where to find a cow, nor why he picked me instead of a more experienced native sailor. How would I get a cow to the ship? Toward that end I coiled a ten foot length of rope over my shoulders. Then, sticking a machete in my belt for the dual purposes of path clearer and weapon, I rowed ashore.

Someone gave me directions to a small farm five miles away where they said a cow <u>might</u> be had. I use the word 'directions' literally, for in a country without roads it is virtually impossible to give more than a compass point coupled with a few geographical landmarks. Thus, the information went like this: go west until you come to a river, not the dry one, but the one that has water. Go upstream until you see the place where there is a bamboo bridge. Cross the bridge but be careful, the bamboo is sometimes slippery. On the other side is a path into the forest. Watch out for big snakes.

Follow the path for about three kilometers, and then you will see the house in a banana grove.

I found the river, the one with the water, crossed the bridge, a rickety affair six bamboos wide with a rope for a handrail, and entered the forest. I saw no snakes, no moving ones that is, but among the ferns and vines it was impossible to distinguish a motionless python from an arm thick *liana*. Sticking carefully to the trail I looked sharply in all directions. It was my first experience in the jungle. Despite the heat which was oppressive and fatiguing, I shivered occasionally. Above me the trees formed a thick canopy with only a minimum of green light filtering through the heavy foliage. The atmosphere was stagnant, like the air in a hot, humid cellar. The ground was spongy with decaying vegetation. Here and there I saw a gorgeous orchid, quite out of place in the monotonous greenery, fastened to a vine-choked tree, feeding upon its unwilling helpless host like a leech on a man's arm.

At the sound of a muffled scream I stopped, goosebumps forming on my skin. Drawing my bolo, I looked around, momentarily expecting some hairy creature to drop on me. But the dense foliage hid whatever made the noise. When there was no further manifestation of danger, I drew a deep but somewhat shaky breath and marched on. Silently I cursed the skipper for sending me on so perilous a mission. A band of monkeys swung by. From tiny babies hanging to their mothers' shaggy breasts to mean-looking, bad-tempered oldsters three feet tall, they screeched, grunted, and paused frequently to scratch or eat. This probably explained the scream. I stopped and relaxed a bit.

Without warning the jungle ended, and I found myself at the edge of a small clearing. It was actually little more than a bog, for here and there I saw stagnant pools of scum-covered water. I was no more than three steps into it when it suddenly became alive with monsters; great reptiles at least six feet long, with shiny, brown-green bodies and slender legs and tails. I had never seen anything so large on land and thought the reptiles might be a species of crocodile. As I stood there, ankle deep in ooze, trying not to move, wave upon wave of ice water ran down my back and sweat dripped from my chin. After their initial panic, the monsters settled down again, moving only at the approach of some flying or crawling insect. I finally realized they weren't crocodiles. Absent was the long, ugly snout, the scaly back and tail, the short legs of the crocodile. The terrible beasts were only giant lizards. The cold wavelets on my back subsided; the jelly firmed in my knees. I stopped sweating and moved forward, cautiously at first, then boldly, right through the middle of the monsters. I found the trail on the far side of the bog, and a few minutes later I stood at the edge of the jungle and saw the house among the banana trees, the house that "might" have a cow.

A bare-breasted young woman sat on a rough bench before the house nursing a naked infant. The sight disconcerted me, and I stopped short. She smiled and nodded and beckoned with her free hand. There was no one else around, but from the distance came the faint yelling of playing children. The woman said something in the vernacular which I did not understand. Then, standing, she shifted the child to her other breast and entered the house. She returned presently with a glass of water. I drank greedily, then handed the empty glass to her, nodding my thanks. She placed the glass on the bench beside her and switched the infant back again. Averting my gaze, I sat near her, trying to disguise my embarrassment.

The sun was halfway down when the husband arrived. To my relief, he spoke a little English. No, he had no cow for sale, not anymore. Besides, how had I expected to get the animal to the ship? I fingered my rope, a bit sheepishly. He laughed and shook his head. Then he gave me a few bananas and sent me on my way. "They might have a cow," indeed.

As we made our slow way southward my English improved steadily. I read and re-read the books in our meager library -- Beau Geste, White Shadows in the South Seas, John Carter of Mars, Captain Salvation. The last book I read only once, being thoroughly disappointed with the hero, a tough sailing ship skipper who, after years of unbridled lust and wickedness, accepted Christ as his Savior and, quite disgustingly, in my opinion, became as gentle as a lamb, dedicating his remaining years to missionary work.

So perfect, in my eyes, became my command of the English tongue that on one occasion I had the temerity to correct the skipper, with embarrassing results. A further blow to my linguistic pride came the following night. Before going ashore, we drew on our accumulated wages from the captain. These he kept in a black box which rang an alarm bell when picked up by dishonest hands.

"How much?" asked the skipper when my turn came.

I shrugged and said, "Oh, a couple of pesos." To my chagrin, for I planned to make a number of purchases at the Chinese *tienda*, he handed me two one-peso bills. I expected five or six. Upon commenting to my shipmates about skipper's stinginess with my money, I was informed that "a couple" means <u>two</u> and no more.

I have always found a certain comfort in the one thing that is common to all the islands from Batanes to Sulu, a common denominator so to speak -- the Chinese store. That sometimes elaborate, more often dingy, establishment is the backbone of island commerce. Without it there would be little trade in the Philippines, indeed, in the whole of Southwest Asia. Later, as the tide of nationalism washed across Asia, the stores disappeared. Under a guided democracy which excludes foreigners, they couldn't survive. This is a pity, for the Chinese traders have done much for the economies of the countries they are in, in addition to keeping the prices at a tolerable level. But in those days, the Chinese store reigned practically supreme. The Filipino store would come, linger a few months, then disappear while its Chinese counterpart endured and flourished from generation to generation. The reasons were simply that of indolence on the part of one and boundless energy on the part of the other. The Chinese had everything, soy sauce, kerosene, dry goods, corned beef, wine, incense and, in the larger towns, even a gasoline pump. And what he did not have, old Ah Gong or young Chua Yu would get. But there was another, vital reason why the Chinese store prospered and the Filipino's withered and perished -- credit. The latter, unable to grant it, was compelled to insist on not always available cash, the former, often backed by an association, just nodded, grinned, and wrote name and amount in a greasy, tattered book.

There was yet another reason for the popularity of the Chinese *tienda*. The experience is my own, but it was duplicated a thousand times every day from Luzon to Malaya. Clutching a wilted peso bill one hot, humid evening, I entered a Filipino store in search of a bottle of cream soda. The price, three centavos. When I handed the money to the young woman behind the counter, she shook her head. No change. I returned the bottle and walked across the street to the Chinese store. He took my peso and, finding not enough change in the drawer, disappeared behind the curtain that separated the store from his meager quarters. I don't know where he got the change, from a hidden coconut shell, or from under his mat, or maybe from a small hoard wrapped in a handkerchief. At any rate, I got my ninety-seven centavos, and he got my business.

The Filipino's *mañana* philosophy, his <u>time</u> -- usually half an hour late for an appointment -- has its charm, and even I could see a definite advantage in mastering time instead of being mastered by it. Few people owned watches in those days and indeed none were needed in a country where time was relative, where a quick squint at the sun sufficed. When the sun rose, it was time to prepare the breakfast; when the house gave no shade, it was noon; and when the red globe hung above the western horizon, suppertime was at hand. Between those three events, telling the time was easy, accurate to the half hour, accurate enough. During the night, time mattered even less, for everyone was asleep. The first pink rays of morning crept through the cracks in the huts and woke the sleepers, starting the cycle anew. What a simple thing time can be; how complicated we make it.

The medical team was exceedingly busy as jungle grapevine, in the form of runner or drum, spread the word. Not so the evangelistic segment of our enterprise, and the fervent prayers and supplications were many, as day followed sterile day. Here and there a church with a congregation of five or six believers was established. But it was no secret that the skipper himself had little hope that it would grow very much or indeed would even exist a year later. Ideally, an evangelist should be left with each newly established congregation, to guide, to teach, to admonish. But qualified evangelists were scarce during those early days. Consequently, on many a bright morning the yacht sailed slowly seaward, leaving a tight little knot of people holding new Bibles which, more often than not, they could barely read.

But our paramount objective, that first voyage, was exploration, an opening of doors, as it were, in order that others might know what to expect. As Captain Skolfield occasionally said, we should be prepared, as we seek to bring the Gospel to the "uttermost parts of the earth." To that end, I think we succeeded admirably. The proof lies in the many churches that have sprung up throughout Palawan and the islands of the Sulu Sea.

Before departing Manila, the ship was fumigated. Even so, as the months passed, it became infested. The fetid heat and darkness spawned numerous creatures of the tropics. Every load of firewood, every bunch of bananas, every basket of mangoes brought scorpions, spiders, centipedes, even snakes.

The dark recesses of bilges, lockers and storerooms swarmed with cockroaches. One morning, as I poured myself a cup of coffee, the flow of liquid from the spout ceased abruptly although the pot was still heavy. Removing the lid, I peered into the pot and promptly decided to forego my second cup. A well-boiled cockroach clogged the opening.

Fishing, except during a full moon or heavy weather was often good, although the fish did not compare to their cold-water relatives in taste or size. Tropical seas are relatively deficient in plankton, the main source of food for marine life. This lack of plankton is directly proportionate to the upwelling of deep, nutrient-laden water that occurs when, as in colder latitudes, the chilled surface water sinks and displaces the warmer lower layers toward the surface.

But it was meat that we craved. What little meat we had consisted of an occasional chicken or a few kilos of carabao meat. Fruits, however, were always available, and the most readily available was the banana. Their shape ranged from the rod-straight to the almost semi-circular, the sizes from short-and-thick to long-and-thin; from the size of a finger to almost the diameter of a forearm; and they came in a variety of colors: almost-white, yellow, red, green, brown.

During the first week in August we cleared the southern tip of Palawan and headed for the island of Buksuk across the choppy North Balabac Strait. We anchored off a small village on the island's eastern coast in mid-afternoon. As always, after a quick glance shoreward, I turned my attention to the depths below the ship. No matter how lovely a panorama might be, how paradisiacal a setting, a land scene is like a painting, majestic perhaps, and breathtaking, or soft and tranquil. But it is motionless. Were you to live a thousand years, the hills would still be there, and the valleys, perhaps even the trees. How different it is below the surface of the ocean, a world of never ending weaving and wafting, of pushing and pulsing, of darting and dashing. Leaning over the rail that

drowsy afternoon, I marveled anew at the fairyland below. The ship seemed to hover in the crystal-clear atmosphere above a strange planet. Not four fathoms below, coral mansions grew from the sea bed, corals of green and red, of blue and orange, or black and white. Each was a great monument to countless billions of tiny polyps whose skeletons slowly but steadily make up its foundation. Among those favored isles, the water is just right for the diminutive creatures to build. If the temperature of the water drops below seventy degrees, they perish from the cold. Below two hundred feet, they drown. In this perfect environment they thrive, and then they die, fashioning their tombs from their own bodies. Here and there, growing from the spiny coral, tall, slender sea plants wafted and swayed in the gentle subsurface currents, harboring myriad fish whose colors and hues matched those of the coral.

Walking to the other side of the ship I looked down. The bottom was sandy. A sandy bottom has an attraction all its own. There rest the giant manta and the shark, huge shapes lying motionless, as if in deep slumber. Or, a ray may soar gracefully above the ocean bed, his great wings stirring up eddies of sand. At night, the sea around the islands glows with mysterious light. Dip your hand into the warm water, and it burns with a cold fluorescent fire. Raise your wet hand, and you can read a newspaper for a few seconds in its light. In the deep, silent fireworks displays go on through the night, quick, sharp streaks of luminescence made by the darting little fishes; shining, undulating waves from sea serpents, solid blobs of fire, stirred up by a shark, a ray, an octopus, or the pulsating, expanding, rippling glow of a jellyfish. The slightest movement, on the surface or below, brings a shower of stars, and the blacker the night, the brighter the fire. The wake of a ship is a mile-long, shimmering train.

Ah Chong had somehow managed to buy a basket of bird's nests and, as amends for a missed lunch in the Strait, made a huge pot of bird's nest soup that evening. The soup was delicious, losing none of its superb flavor even when we were told, while eating, or rather, slurping it, that we were in reality partaking of the saliva which the birds, a species of swallow, exude and which dries on contact with the air, giving the nest a sort of noodle-like appearance. The birds build their nests on towering, almost inaccessible cliffs. But even there they are not safe, for the Chinese value them highly and pay handsomely, making the perilous climbs profitable.

Running down the eastern coast of Balabac Island in a roaring gale, we passed the high-on-a-hill Balabac Light, the Cape Melville Light on the southeast tip, and crossed the tumultuous Balabac Strait. We skirted the Great Danger

Bank, the Mangaree Great Reef, and numerous smaller reefs, where sudden death on the razor sharp coral and snake infested waters threatened ship and crew alike.

My heart beat high as I pored over the chart of the Borneo coast. Because of the incessant squalls I had yet to glimpse my fabled island. How eagerly my fingers traced the coast and the neighboring islands and shoals as I silently read their names, which shouted adventure and romance in my imagination: Monmouth Shoals, Wanderer Shoal, Marchesa Bank, Royalist Rock, Minna Reefs, Nymphe Rock, Driftwood Point...

The Islands of the Sulu Sea

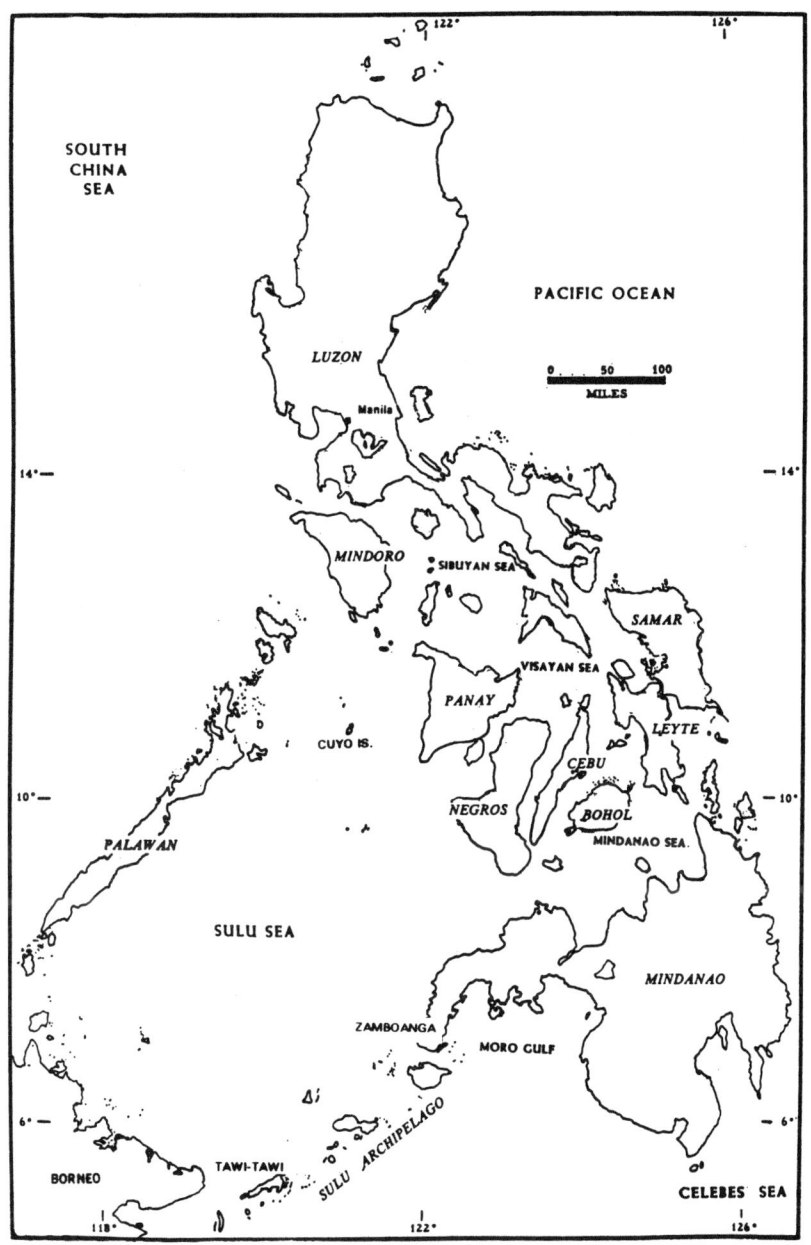

The Philippines and the Sulu Sea, home to the Gospel Ship and myself for many years.

15

Borneo

Our trip to Borneo was not for missionary reasons. Foreign-flag vessels operating in the Philippines must clear through a non-Philippine port at least once a year. Getting a clearance from Borneo would allow us to spend another year in the Islands.

When I went on watch at 8 p.m., it was still drizzling. Peering intently into the darkness, trying to see the island of my dreams, I saw only more darkness. An hour later, the engine room telegraph clanged harshly. I stopped the engine. The telegraph clanged again. I put the engine in reverse. I felt the anchor chain race through the hawsepipe. When the telegraph pointer dropped to "stop," I throttled down. The chief engineer came down with the news that rather than risk the ship on one of the many reefs that lay between us and our destination, the skipper wanted to wait for daylight.

Finishing my chores, I then hurried on deck, expecting to see only drizzly darkness. Stepping into the night, I stopped in my tracks, looking around in wonder. The rain had stopped. A few scattered clouds drifted across the sky. The shore of Borneo lay barely a mile away, its jungles illuminated by the setting moon. In the years to come, I would thrill to many a sight but none was as vivid as that still night when I stared at the land whose very name had intrigued me since I first saw an orangutan in the Dresden Zoo. Gazing at the dark landscape, I actually trembled with excitement. How mysterious the jungle looked, bathed in the eerie red light of the moon, how hostile and deadly, yet how inviting. My eyes roamed up and down the coast. Not a light showed, not the faintest glimmer, and when the moon, after briefly outlining the irregular silhouette of the forest, sank, the land looked absolutely black, blending almost perfectly with the slightly less black water.

I tossed restlessly through the remainder of the night, and was on deck with the dawn. Shivering a little in the dank, cold air, I stepped to the rail and looked shoreward. The jungle was still dark but had already lost the inky blackness of the night. Far to the south west, a high mountain stabbed through layers of pink cloud, its flank still enveloped in darkness, its tip blazing red-gold.

Throughout the day we ran along the northern coast on

a southeasterly course. I stood at the starboard rail every free minute of that day. The water's edge was thickly lined with mangroves whose dark, gnarled roots, like bony arms and legs, clutched the slimy bottom, forming a bulwark against the ever growing, ever pushing jungle behind. This perspective of the Borneo coast was monotonous, with never a break in the incredibly green maze. Yet, there were people in that green mass. I could see the smoke from their cooking fires, columns of grey smoke that barely rose above the top of the trees, then spread out as if flowing beneath an invisible ceiling. As the ship slipped through the oily-smooth water, I wondered about those people. Could they be human at all, living in that thick, dank jungle of trees, vines and miasmatic swamps? Or were they still existing on the lower level of the evolutionary pyramid, half man, half beast? Vision after vision tumbled through my mind. I sought, in vain, to get a glimpse of the ape-men I read about in books authored by men and women who had never been closer to Borneo than the orangutan cage at the local zoo. But I knew no better. Thus, my imagination made the most of my ignorance. Having rejected the Biblical account of the creation under the competent tutelage of my father and my teacher, there remained no reference for me. I could only speculate on man's beginning, in the dim and totally uncertain light of science.

As the sun set, we rounded the sandstone cliffs of Balhalla, standing in toward crowded Sandakan harbor. Wherever the eye roved, something was in motion — wheezy little steam launches, a diesel tug with a tow, sampans, a pair of Moro *vintas*, small junks, a log-laden *batil*. Some of the vessels tried crossing the yacht's path at the last possible moment, as if tempting the various gods associated with the different crafts.

I requested permission to remain on deck during our entrance into the harbor. Consequently, even when I heard the faint clanging of the engine room telegraph and the answering jingle on the bridge, I stayed glued to my vantage point in the bow. The yacht, deprived of the powerful thrust of the screw, slowed rapidly. Even as she slowed, a yellow and white launch detached itself from the harbor traffic and sped toward us. In a wicker chair on the short foredeck sat a stocky white man. His pith helmet lay on the deck beside him. In one hand he held a glass, with the other he fanned himself furiously. The craft made a wide sweep, coming behind our slowly gliding ship. In another minute it was made fast at the gangway. Carefully placing his glass on the deck, the pilot got to his feet, gripped the fan with his teeth, and hoisted himself to the gangway platform. He eyed the creaking fall rope dubiously, then hurried up the eight steps.

We anchored a short distance from the fairway. The Customs, Quarantine, and Immigration offices were closed for the day, so we couldn't go farther. The pilot clambered down the bridge ladder, down the gangway and into his launch without missing a wave of his fan, and the boat roared off toward the wooden wharf half a mile away.

My eyes traveled across the intervening strip of water to the shore where naked children chased one another on the rickety, smoke-enveloped walkways connecting the squalid huts built on stilts over the muddy harbor water. Beyond the first few streets, the rest of the town straggled up a steep hillside behind the harbor. At a certain level, as if on command — and I guessed that it *was* a command — the mean houses stopped. Beyond, smothered in Bougainvillea and Flame-of-the-Forest trees, nestled the bungalows of the whites and perhaps other opulent segments of the populace. To my left, and somewhat lower, a large, squat building surrounded by a wide veranda overlooked the harbor. That must be the inevitable Planter's Club I had heard so much about.

Already, in 1932, the tide of freedom was rising in the Far East. India was beginning to fret, as was Burma, and the Philippines. Borneo was one of the few areas in the Orient where King George still held absolute sway. The King and

The Company, that is, the North Borneo Trading Company. There was still a lot of starch in the colonial spirit. The white man still died in the big island's fever-drenched jungles, or in his house amid the rubber trees or under the coconut palms. He did so for the glory of England and the profit of The Company. But there were fewer every year, even in Borneo. North Borneo was still a Crown Colony, however, and its rulers allowed no one, white or brown, to forget it. We were not there two days before I was quite curtly reminded that my white skin had its prerogatives and privileges.

We tied up at the wharf at 10 o'clock the following morning. Fifteen minutes later I stood, barefoot and thrilled, on the rough wharf planks. At last, after years of longing, I stood on Borneo's soil. Abruptly, as I strode up and down the wharf, I realized that I was standing not on land at all, but on a wharf. Stealthily, for I had no permission, I rounded the shed and ran toward the street. There I stopped under a sign informing me that I was on the street called Yalan Tiga. Placing my bare feet squarely on the dirty cobblestones, I took a deep breath of garlic flavored air. After a few moments I hurried back to the ship.

Supper was tasteless, not because of the cooking but due to my excitement. I put on my best almost-white shirt, a suit of the same color, and shoes. The latter, I had liberally doused with liquified chalk, then sprinkled and rubbed with talcum powder to give them a sheen. In my pocket was a five peso bill, plus a few coins. The Yalan Tiga presented a rather dismal appearance, but what it lacked in elegance, it more than made up for in its exotic ambiance. A more sophisticated man, or one less imbued with the spirit of romance, might have viewed the unkempt scene with distaste, but I was, if not exactly in paradise, at least quite close to it.

Both sides of the street were lined with shops, bars, and refreshment parlors — all doing brisk business. Here and there a family sat in front of a dark door, enjoying the coolness of the evening. The narrow sidewalks were crowded as Hindus, Chinese, Malays, Dyaks and at least one young, wide-eyed Westerner pressed and jostled and pushed along. As in Hong Kong, the streetwalkers were much in evidence, only a little bolder — doll-like Chinese girls in black blouses and pantaloons, slender Malays in short, tight dresses, all walking slowly, with sinuous movements and frank glances.

At a sidewalk bookstore I bought a book entitled, *No Other Tiger*. At a tailor's shop I haggled for a pair of overalls and a shirt. And in another bookstall I purchased a postcard picturing a very lightly-clad Dyak girl, addressing it then and there to my sister. A pair of tennis shoes finished my purchases and most of my money. Thus laden, I walked slowly toward the harbor. On an impulse, I turned into a narrow side street, intending to return to the Yalan Tiga a block farther down. The street, a mere alley, was dark save for an occasional yellow beam of light from an unshuttered window. I was halfway down the block when I realized that, far from being deserted, the street was actually alive with shadowy forms which, seeking the still-darker shadows of the houses, shuffled almost noiselessly along. Now and then a door opened suddenly, admitting a black-clad figure and closed as quickly. I lengthened my strides, clutching my bundles a little tighter. Once, as I hurried past a door, it flew open, and despite my apprehension, I slowed my steps. The room was large, illuminated by a dim, unshaded electric bulb. A row of double tiered bunks lined the only wall I could see. As the door closed behind an entering patron, a cloud of unpleasantly-sweet odor swirled around me. Opium! I hurried on, my heart in my throat, a prickly sensation crawling up and down my back. Abruptly, as in Hong Kong — only more realistically, for the setting was even more appropriate — Fu Man Chu's evil face rose before me. In the distance behind me I could still see the relative brightness of the Yalan Tiga, but instead of turning back, I continued, albeit at an accelerated pace. It was hot and humid; the stagnant air lay in an odorous blanket over the dark alley. The predominant smell was that sickening sweetness, relieved now and then by a familiar and, therefore, more pleasant odor — garlic. From some deep recess and barely audible came the discordant strains of a Chinese fiddle and the faint, sharp clicking of mah-jongg tiles. As I turned the first corner, the sound of feminine laughter slowed my steps once more. Peering through the partially-shuttered window I gasped at the carnal scene within; then ran all the way back to the Yalan Tiga. Still a little shaken, I entered a refreshment parlor and ordered a soft drink. Sipping the tepid soda, I reconstructed the past few minutes during which I came face to face with quite another aspect of Oriental life, an atmosphere of evil beyond belief, the nether world of opium and lust.

Finishing my drink, I picked up my parcels and continued walking, becoming increasingly aware of the curious stares of the people I met. Even more blatant were the looks of those still sitting before their houses. An old Chinese crone pointed at me and made a comment which caused those near her to smile. Looking at my clothing, I expected a tear or a large spot, but found nothing amiss. I walked faster and finally reached the ship, breathless and uneasy.

The following morning, a shipyard engineer came aboard to repair a piece of machinery. I offered to bring the piece to the shipyard later that day, whereupon his eyebrows rose.

"Do you mean you intend to carry it yourself?" he asked.

I nodded. It was not very heavy nor large.

He frowned, then said sternly. "A white man never carries a burden. Please bear this in mind. Let one of the natives carry it for you, a few paces behind you."

Now I knew the reason behind the stares and comments the previous night. I was carrying my own parcels.

The sticky Borneo night was descending when the three of us, the chief mate, the chief engineer, and I walked up the

Yalan Tiga toward the Club. It was supposed to be a dinner, the chief paying, but it turned out to be something quite different for me. As we slowly climbed, the atmosphere became less sticky, due, not so much to the slightly higher altitude but to the abundance of trees and shrubs. The odors of dried fish, garlic, horse manure, wood smoke, in short, the smells of a tropical town on a hot night, were replaced with the fragrance of frangipangi and countless other blossoms. This added to the illusion of great distance between town and hill, although they were barely a mile apart.

A bowing, white-clad Malay greeted us at the wide doors of the high-ceilinged dining room. The low murmur of voices stopped momentarily, then resumed.

Dinner was fair but the service excellent. I ate little, being content to watch the waiters hasten noiselessly from table to bar and back again. Overhead, huge fans kept the air moving, their soft swishing blending perfectly with the murmur of the conversation around us. There were no women present, the ratio being twenty to one among the white population. The men were mostly young, but here and there a white-haired head stood out in the soft light. Not everyone wore coat or tie. This diminished some of the glamour I expected at a Planter's Club. But the fact that I was among the Builders of Empires, breathing the same air, eating the same food, and gazing at their deeply-tanned faces, more than compensated for the slight disillusion. I was supremely happy.

Dinner over, we strolled to an adjoining room and took our seats at a wide, open window. Below us lay the town; the short, fairly bright ribbon of the Yalan Tiga, the dimly lit alleys that crisscrossed the town, the dull, flickering lights on the small river and coastal craft in the harbor and the bright cluster lights on the Singapore-Kudat-Jesselton-Sandakan motorship *Marudu*.

A young chap in a white merchant marine officer uniform approached our table and introduced himself. His name was R. Caisson Keen. He was the third engineer on the *Marudu*. After having a drink with us, he asked, "I say, won't you join me for dinner on board tomorrow? Half-past five?"

As the minutes flowed into hours, I found the room becoming warmer. This vaguely disturbed me since I knew it usually gets cooler as night advances. Also, the polished floor seemed to be heaving when I stood up to wander about a bit. I tried, unsuccessfully, to fathom the problem. I had only a little to drink, or so I thought, a few beers, a couple of stingers, a glass of wine, a little rum, all suggested and eagerly supplied by my two solicitous shipmates.

Walking back to the ship, I almost fell off the wharf. Falling into my bunk, babbling gleefully, I immediately fell asleep. The sun was high when I awoke. Bathed in sweat and vomit, I shuddered and groaned, wishing I could die. The chief engineer very graciously excused me from work, then, grinning, he patted my clenched fist and left me to my misery. The episode, whatever the two chiefs may have had in mind, left me with a healthy distaste for alcohol.

The following afternoon, after recovering and very glad to be alive after all, I determined to see a little more of Borneo. Renting a somewhat dilapidated bicycle of unknown origin from a small rental shop, I headed for the back country. For a short distance the road was paved. This gave way to a tarred surface which then became dusty, narrowing all the while. The jungle was thick on both sides, forming a dark green ceiling over the road. I pedaled on in the joyous knowledge that my heart's desire was fulfilled. Occasionally I stopped as a screech or a roar fell on my ears, but the dense jungle revealed none of its secrets and I was afraid to leave the road.

The first inkling I had of the lateness of the hour was not a look at my watch, for I had none, nor a squint at the sun, because I could not see it, but the increasing number of people hurrying toward town. The darker it became the faster

The Islands of the Sulu Sea

they walked. The men, barefoot and wearing shorts and singlets, both for the most part tattered and sweat-stained, carried farm implements on their shoulders. The women were mostly elderly. There were a few young ones who looked surprisingly pretty, walking with a grace that their western sisters could do well to emulate. Most of the women carried produce piled high on their heads. A few youngsters, naked save for a navel length singlet, plodded alongside the women, quickly moving to the opposite side upon seeing me.

Loath to turn back, I went on until I could hardly distinguish the stones on the road. Then I stopped and looked about me. Suddenly I was afraid. In the gathering darkness the jungle looked black, alien and hostile. Quickly turning around, I pedaled rapidly back, beset by all manner of thoughts, thoughts that remained hidden during the daylight hours but now came slithering forth in the dark. The jungle seemed to close in on me. As I wheeled through a particularly dark tunnel of foliage, I felt real terror, expecting momentarily to be transfixed by a headhunter's spear or arrow. I didn't know at the time that headhunters fear the night, too. Why, I mused, had the natives hurried so, if no danger lurked on the lonely road? I remembered pictures, photographs, of Dyak longhouses, the doors and windows decorated with human skulls. Would my own blond head grace some hut that very night? I wondered, shivered and peddled frantically. My imagination ranged to pythons and haradryads, flying snakes and rabid bats, all of which I knew inhabited my dream island. But what terrified me the most, what raised the gooseflesh on my arms, were the spirits that roamed the forest. I had recently read a book on the jungle spirits of the Burmese that captured my imagination and seemed quite believable. As I glanced fearfully at the forest, the malevolent gods, the sprites, the witches, were real, indeed, leering from the blackness, whispering, hissing, sighing, darkly mumbling. It was with a great sense of relief that I spied the first feeble light. Human presence, I thought with relief. Half an hour later I coasted to a stop before the bicycle shop and returned the bicycle to the old Chinese. Mopping my brow, I walked, still a little shaky, but invigorated, to the harbor.

16

Sulu

We sailed early the following day. When the sun went down, our anchor splashed into the motionless water off Sitankai, the southern-most piece of Philippine soil and Port of Entry for traffic from Celebes, Java, and Borneo.

Sitankai is surrounded by a wide, shallow shelf, so shallow that at low tide the water is only knee-deep. It was strange to see the island youngsters cavorting a mile from the shore.

Following a quick visit to the lonely house of the customs officer the next morning, we were soon on our way north. Ahead lay the notorious and lovely Tawi-tawi Islands, the haunts of pirates and smugglers, the islands of the Moros. This is not to say the inhabitants were all smugglers or pirates anymore than one would call all people from Chicago gangsters. But the Sulu Moros were nevertheless once the most feared pirates in the East, outranked only by their brethren of the China Coast. The Moro forays into Celebes and Borneo are legion and well-documented. No vessel was safe from attack unless it could outsail the swift *kumpits* and *vintas*, an almost impossible task. The "trade" continued in the 30's. Even today, smuggling and piracy still exist in the outer reaches of these islands.

After a somewhat rough crossing of the Sibutu Passage, we skirted the island of Simunul, anchoring for the night off its southern tip. This, despite the swift current and poor holding ground. About noon the next day, we passed the Bongao Light, and shortly thereafter made fast at the old wooden wharf. A sizeable crowd, composed mostly of men and children, gathered on the wharf to stare at the yacht and us. We stood staring at the town and them.

I soon discovered after leaving Manila that white men could be found in the most unexpected places in the islands. But, more often than not, the sight of them filled me with dismay. I became ashamed of my own race when I beheld the sodden, bleary-eyed, almost toothless, though by no means old, derelicts. More often than not they lived in utter obscurity, surrounded by their dirty, half-naked offspring and unkempt native wives. Their only mementos of a better and more useful life were photographs, often elaborately framed but always slightly yellowed by age and heat. These remembrances were always in evidence as if to remind themselves and the infrequent visitors that there had been better days. Usually the photo depicted a strapping young man in an army uniform, a neat little frame house with a white picket fence around it, or a pretty girl on the steps of a streetcar. For a few minutes, or an hour, while we sat slowly rocking on some rickety porch, dull eyes brightened, wrinkles softened and thin lips relaxed in a dreamy smile, as the ex-soldier or the ex-sailor, reminisced — of his native Iowa or "Frisco" before and after the 'quake, of the Battle of Manila Bay, "where the Dons didn't have no chance, the moment The Admiral give the word." But all too often, at the sound of a strident, scolding voice inside the house, the old-timer would heave a slow sigh, the dreamy look would fade, the words dry up. Then I would leave, disturbed and depressed, wondering if I, too, would some day be like that, disillusioned, disgusted, seeking solace and forgetfulness in drink.

But there were exceptions, notable exceptions, who buoyed me up and renewed my faith in my race. I met one not long after we left Manila. His name was Wallace. A ship's captain and a veteran of the Spanish-American War, he was tall, slightly stooped, with a large nose, and deeply-tanned and leathery face. With a little money, much determination, and aided by an intelligent, personable Filipina wife, he had literally hewn himself a small lumber empire from the thick forests of western Palawan. His ships carried a variety of timber through the China and Sulu Seas. Sometimes they were loaded with logs so light the ballast tanks were kept full to provide stability. On other occasions the cargo of trees was so heavy and dense that before the ship was half full, she was down to her plimsoll marks. In a day when radio communication was by no means common, all his ships were equipped with a wireless. They kept in constant touch with his house on the hill.

Occasionally he took command of one of his ships. Good-natured rumor had it that the ship he commanded usually sunk or foundered. At least three of his ships were known to have gone down. This puzzled me until one night I saw him pilot his ship at near-full speed through a channel so rocky and winding that we always negotiated it at dead-slow speed in daylight.

Captain Skolfield, staring with us into the darkness, put our thoughts to words.

"Wallace must be on the bridge."

An hour later he came on board, grinning broadly and obviously quite pleased with his performance.

It was simply bravado, not a desire for insurance money, that caused him to lose ships.

On one of the many occasions when we met, he slapped my back and in his booming voice expressed his pleasure that I had not yet "kicked the bucket." Still unfamiliar with that particular expression, I merely muttered that I was happy with life aboard the yacht. I had no intention of kicking any bucket. I took him literally.

At Bongao I was to meet another notable exception. As we stood at the railing, contemplating the town, a voice in the rear of the crowd on the wharf shouted, "Tuan Billy."

The people made way for a medium-built white man. He wore somewhat rumpled white pants and shirt. A white pith helmet was pushed back on his head, revealing a good crop of graying hair. Running his hand over his mustache, he approached rapidly, his white tennis shoes contrasting oddly with the bare brown feet of the natives. Without breaking stride, he gripped a shroud line, stepped on the railing and jumped to the deck. We were not long in discovering that this was Wilhelm Schuck, former Deputy Governor of Sulu, planter, trader, husband of a beauteous Moro woman of royal descent, and father of a brood of stalwart sons and lovely daughters. Also, he was a German.

We were further informed that *tuan* Billy, (*tuan* means lord, or master) had already imported a German son-in-law for his eldest daughter. This bit of news was instantly pounced upon by my shipmates; that and the fact that the old gentleman had another younger daughter. It was, therefore, with some trepidation that I answered the skipper's summons to meet the visitor an hour later. As we shook hands I detected, or thought I did, a glint in the German's gray eyes. But I was not carried off that afternoon. Nothing, in fact, was said about the girls or marriage, whatever may have been in our guest's mind.

Bongao is one of the loneliest islands in the Sulu Sea, a mere mountain peak rising sharply from the sea, surrounded by a gleaming ring of white coral sand. Crags and spires thrust into the clouds, and high up on one of these a palm tree clung, somehow fastened to barren rock. The Tree of Life, the old ones said. It had always been there, undisturbed and unmarred by the forces of nature. The Moros believed that if a man could pick its fruit, he would achieve eternal youth. But those who tried, and they were many, found not vigor and life, but death. A single glance at the towering rock convinced me that only a winged creature could reach the ancient tree.

The first objects that met my gaze as I stepped off the rickety pier and walked slowly along, were two graves. They rested on a grassy spot near the crumbling wall of the old Spanish fort and marked the final resting place of two young white soldiers. They were murdered by the notorious pirate Jikiri during the early, hectic days of the American occupation that never quite succeeded in Sulu.

The dusty streets were crowded, as they always are at dusk in the tropics. The men looked ferocious, smiling little but scowling much. Their forbidding demeanor was further accented by broad sashes around their waists holding wicked looking krises. In addition, a few carried thin, long daggers in the sashes. They wore tight trousers split at the feet, with small buttons running up the legs. Many wore vest-like jackets, open at the front, revealing lean, hairless torsos. They constantly chewed betel nut, which gave their mouths the appearance of horrid red gashes in the otherwise dark faces. Their teeth were black and filed, sometimes to mere stumps.

The women presented a more attractive picture. Some of them were exceedingly comely. Dressed in sarong-like garments, they also wore tight, multi-buttoned jackets which made the more buxom ones appear quite constricted and uncomfortable. Their hair was pulled tightly over the scalp and tied in a small bun at the nape. Unlike the men, they smiled often, also revealing betel nut-stained lips and teeth. However, as I walked along, I noticed some of the younger girls had not yet taken up the habit and I found their smiles fetching, indeed.

Warned by those on the ship, I kept a sharp lookout for that occasional scourge of the Sulu Islands, the *juramentado* or "amuck." I learned that out of religious fanaticism, this strange and terrifying creature, always a man, goes berserk. In response to a real or a fancied wrong he shaves his eyebrows and cinches his waistband until breathing becomes difficult. Then, barong or kris held high, and beset with a frenzied bloodlust, he rampages through the streets in search of Christians. His own kind will do if none of the other are available. Leaving behind him a trail of blood and death, his belief is that for each dead follower of Christ the reward is one dark-eyed *houri* in Mohammed's Paradise. It is a suicide mission. The *juramentado* knows that, once he starts, he will quickly die (there is no other way to stop him), and thus he puts all his energy into his fevered spree of wanton murder. His thirteenth Christian, if he gets that far (which few do), entitles him to enter Paradise on a white charger. When he does, the *houris* will be waiting.

I secretly rejoiced in my immunity from such a death. After all I was an atheist, not a Christian. It didn't occur to me that the crazed killer would quite logically assume any white man, unless he knew him personally, was a Christian. Thus I carelessly walked along Bongao's dusty streets, unaware that I had two strikes against me. A *juramentado* might deliberately single me out, not only for being a Christian, which I was not, but which he could not know, and for being white, another thorn in many a brown hide.

My ignorant bliss evaporated when I became more fully acquainted with life in Sulu. It made me less cocky, but didn't dim my liking for the islands.

17

Zamboanga

Almost a year had passed, a year of Bible study, of religious discussion, of memorizing. Seeing men and women stand hip-deep in the sea to be baptized, I knew the reason for baptism as intimately as any Baptist. I knew, too, about the Rapture, the Second Coming, the Holy Spirit, and Satan. I say I knew, for in time a man can learn much. But although my head was packed full of things religious, none of it seeped into my heart. Quite the contrary. Whereas previously I listened most tolerantly to the testimonies to God's love, I soon began to find it increasingly distasteful and made no secret of it. One serene, starry night, as our carpenter extolled the goodness of God, I quite heatedly, if not viciously, suggested he stop giving "your God" the credit for events that would occur without his help anyway. Yet perversely, when someone casually mentioned that any white man contemplating marriage to a Moro girl would perforce have to embrace Islam, it made me shudder, despite the fact that I had no intention of wooing any such dusky damsel.

I rarely contemplated death and then only abstractly. Oblivion was easily understood. A person died, and that was that. Not pleasant, to be sure, but unavoidable. Only once did the thought of death affect me profoundly. Strangely enough, it had nothing to do with dying but with a bright, rain-washed day. As I watched people hurry by, and my eyes took in the blue sky, the white, fluffy clouds, the palm-fringed bay, and the azure water, I felt a sudden sense of loss. All that would still be there when I went to the grave; the people, the sky and sea, the whole beautiful world. But I would be gone. I clenched my hands in sudden fury. How senseless it all seemed. A few years of light and life, then darkness and oblivion. Why was I on earth anyhow? What was the reason for the journey from oblivion to oblivion with so little warmth and joy between?

My thoughts soon turned to other things, but the regret, the self-pity, the sense of loss, haunted me for days afterward.

Mr. Schuck came along when we sailed, a day later. With him was his daughter Amy, a bright-eyed, vivacious and very pretty girl of fifteen. We made our slow way northward, stopping briefly at islands that lay like emeralds on the blue sea, islands with names few white men knew or would ever hear — Sanga-Sanga, Bilatoan, Mantabuan, Tandubas, Siasi. The girl and I were constantly together, under the benevolent eyes of both her father and the skipper. Perhaps our propinquity affected me more than her. When we anchored in Jolo's quiet harbor a few days later and she stood at the gangway, all dressed in white, shading her eyes from the sun as she looked at me, her smile was bright. There was no hint of sadness. I watched her jump lightly into the boat, feeling a happy, wistful glow in my heart.

I saw her again, briefly, that evening as I strolled, alone, along the Chinese pier savoring the coolness and the exotic atmosphere. Until recently this was a place where harem girls and slaves were landed and sold to the highest bidder. Even now a profitable trade in contraband was going on. Rounding a building, I spotted Amy's neat, white-clad form almost instantly. With her were two girls, one tall and haughty of mien, the other somewhat shorter, plumper, and extraordinarily lovely. I later learned the two girls were sisters. The tall one was Jahara who turned out not to be haughty at all, but quite friendly. But it was Maimunah who captivated me instantly. She wore a dress of delicate pink that extended to slightly below the knee and seemed to impart a subtle radiance to her honey-colored skin. Her bare, well-rounded arms were unadorned save for a thin golden band on her left wrist. She was stockingless and even in her medium-high shoes barely reached my shoulders. But it was her face that held my gaze. Her nose was small and straight, her lips red and innocent of make-up and quite devoid of betelnut. Her eyes were large and lustrous, of the deepest black and very, very soft, and, they were riveted on me. We exchanged a greeting. Then the girls continued their promenade. I lacked the presence of mind and audacity to go along. I went my solitary, and now somewhat forlorn, way, suddenly no longer interested in harems and slaves.

We sailed after attending a mid-morning prayer meeting at the small church of the Reverend Mr. Gulbranson of the Christian Missionary Alliance. Seating myself behind a post in a corner in order to remain as inconspicuous as possible, I hoped I wouldn't be asked to pray. I accepted the invitation to the special meeting for only one reason, the hope of seeing the girls again. Unfortunately they didn't attend. In time I would see more, much more of the matchless Tawi-tawi Islands, and the girls, but this I didn't know that morning. And so, as we sailed, I felt real regret and could only sigh and curse the sailor's lot.

We moored our ship at Zamboanga's wide concrete pier in the late afternoon. Zamboanga, nestling beside the blue sea on the western tip of Mindanao, is one of the few really exotic towns in the Philippines. Few cities have more romantic names, and fewer still have seen more romance. Zamboanga! How deliciously the name lies on the tongue. For more than three hundred years Zamboanga was steeped in the heady wine of prose and poetry. Sieges and pirate raids, serenading cavaliers from Spain, stern faced prelates, missionaries, opium smugglers, slave girls, spinster teachers, soldiers and soldiers' wives, gaiety, tragedy, the thunder and frenzy of battle, the peace of the tropics. They all spell Zamboanga. Her palm-lined streets have echoed men's exuberant laughter and women's quiet weeping, the rattle of armor and the blare of trumpets.

Lovely women abound in Zamboanga, and as I watched the never-ending promenade of beautiful girls in twos and threes down the broad avenue in the cool of the evening, I knew the storytellers spoke the truth. The girls, dressed fetchingly in simple apparel, were light of skin, straight of nose, and regal of carriage. They talked softly, and their frequent giggling was like the tinkling of silver bells. They strolled to the edge of the pier, cast interested and sometimes coquettish glances our way, then returned slowly, stately, to the town by way of the wide street. It was a sight almost beyond description — the brilliant sunset clouds, the blue sea, the green palm trees, the white pier, the pastel-colored dresses of the promenading girls, all enveloped in a gentle, fragrant breeze.

We took on fuel and water during the night and were gone, "...ere the soft rays of the rising sun caressed the fair faces..." of the beauteous, sleeping Zamboanga belles. Alas, the sailor's life.

We were six hours out of Zamboanga, on a northwesterly course, when we ran into a gale so ferocious that at the first vicious gust the yacht heeled far to port. The force of the wind increased rapidly, raising stupendous waves. The ship shuddered as blow upon blow fell on her flanks; her timbers groaned under the sustained straining and twisting as she was flung into a trough, then dragged to a crest and dropped once more. The tall, raked masts whipped in concert, and the taut shrouds twanged like the strings on a fiddle. It seemed only a matter of time before the ship's back would break under the incessant hammering and wrenching, and leave her a derelict, at the mercy of the wild sea. In the engine room, it was virtually impossible to stand upright on the heaving, slippery floorplates surrounded by hot metal. One instant of inattention and a person could skitter into the huge, spinning flywheel, or mangle his foot in the grinding eccentrics. Yet, move around one must, for the safety of the ship and its crew in a storm lies as much in the engineer's hands as it does the captain's. If the engine fails, even for a few minutes, the ship may capsize. Thus, certain functions must be carried out unfailingly. Oil levels must be checked, bearings greased, filters cleaned or changed, temperatures watched. And at all times, a hand must be on the throttle to hold back the racing horses when the propeller loses its bite as the stern is flung skyward, lest the engine tear itself from the bedplate. Then, when the bow points at the churning clouds and the stern buries itself in the sea, the throttle must quickly be opened, lest the diesel stop under the sudden load.

When the gale broke, our distance was seventy miles from the island of Cagayancillo, a speck on the chart in the middle of the Sulu Sea, a mere seven hour run in good weather. But three full days and nights were to go by before, on a dismal morning, the island came in sight. Three days and nights of misery, of howling and roaring, of never-ending motion, until sanity hung on a slender thread and every cell ached for release from the endless pounding.

We ran past the island, then swung in a great arc to approach it. Whereas the ship had previously met the seas head-on, she was now running before them. Wave after wave roared over the stern, or lifted the ship high, raced under her, then flung her down. Almost abruptly it seemed, we were in quieter water, and half an hour later, at anchor. Damage was minor, some broken crockery, a smashed window, a scalded hand, and the inevitable water damage as deck seams opened or a porthole leaked.

The island of Cagayancillo, although it is not even shown on world maps, and is isolated in the center of the Sulu Sea, was not at all backward, being serviced by a bi-monthly coastwise steamer. There was an adequate school, a hospital of sorts, and, of course, a Roman Church. Thus, while our arrival was noticed, it stirred little excitement. But the island nonetheless struck me as a dreary place, not one where I would have liked to spend a great deal of time, let alone live.

Although our evangelists preached day and night, visiting homes, standing on the streets, or distributing tracts, they had little success. But Captain Skolfield was happy enough, cheerfully talking of "the seed sown." His words, apparently a standard expression in evangelical circles, were received with much wise and solemn nodding. To me it sounded strange and ineffective.

On the day before we were to sail, all of us received an invitation to a dance at the school. Many of us, myself included, accepted. Clad in my finest, which was not very fine, I stepped into the crew's quarters an hour after dinner. A half dozen young men were putting on the last, oily touches to hair and eyebrows. Before the single, cracked mirror stood a sailor named Leonardo, a man extraordinarily well-versed in the art of courting, if nothing else. In the year we were under way, he became engaged no less than four times in four different places. Thus far, the yacht had not touched any of the places twice. But speculation ran high and was eagerly awaited at what would happen if Leonardo were confronted by his forsaken loves. The fact that he was something of a dandy and a rather fancy dresser were the probable reasons for his successes for he was not overly handsome. As he finished knotting his tie, he turned to pick up his coat. I stared, open-mouthed. The front of his snow-white shirt was crisp and smooth, while the back was bare except for a strip of shoulder and the tail. The rest of his shirt was gradually eaten away by perspiration during his many sultry nights of wooing. Seeing my incredulous stare, he grinned and shrugged, whereupon two other sailors took off their coats to show similar attire. Suddenly I knew why, no matter how hot and sticky the night, Leonardo never removed his coat when he was ashore. It was his only shirt.

The dance was a dreary affair, but a welcome change. I had never before attempted the art of the dance but a comely lass of sixteen or thereabouts, bare of leg and short of skirt, caught my fancy. I bowed boldly and took her hand before she had time to shake her head. Across the room our Leonardo, suave and beaming, was wooing his girl via the old and so effective method of charming the mother, who sat beside her. His three gold teeth gleamed in the light of the Coleman lanterns. My partner was only slightly more adept than I in the tricky steps. We must have presented a ludicrous picture. But it didn't matter. Everyone else was either dancing or engaged in lively conversation. I was content to hold the lissome girl even though, halfway through the dance, her thin blouse began to stick to her moist skin under my hand. There was a bowl of tepid punch and a large platter of rather dry and crumbly cookies. The punch was quickly gone, for the night was hot. The cookies were ignored. After two more rounds, my fair partner ditched me for someone better versed in the tango, and I sat down on one of the many chairs against the wall and watched. When we left at daybreak, Leonardo was still wearing his coat and I realized I never learned my partner's name.

18

Return to Manila

We entered Manila Bay during the night. From the thick darkness, ten miles away, the city looked like a jewel. I had seen only feeble lights during the previous year. A mere handful of towns in the southern islands had electric lights, and those were mainly of the 25 watt variety. An entire town of five thousand people might use less electricity than a single metropolitan city block. I forgot how bright a city could be, and that night I was no less impressed by the lights than any savage confronted by a 50 watt bulb.

Our anchorage was the same as fifty-four weeks earlier, just off the Manila Hotel. After setting the telegraph to "finished with engines," I hurried on deck to sit on the rail and gaze at the city of light. The fragrance and the soft music that drifted to the ship on the wings of an offshore breeze were an exotic delight.

Nordstrom, the chief engineer, taken shortly before he left the ship to take a mining job in the mountains of Luzon. From the author's collection.

A few days later, both the chief engineer and the chief officer left the yacht, unable to face another long voyage, with its attendant monotony, its loneliness, its uncertainties. The engineer obtained a position with a mining firm in the mountain province of Luzon. He speedily wired his wife and daughter to join him. Mr. Farjoe, the mate, boarded a ship for Shanghai, where he soon became skipper of a China coaster, a job infinitely more to his liking than working on a missionary ship. He filled me with many tales of the China Coast. He knew the closely-knit, rough and ruddy lot who were the real bosses of the coast, whose word was law on the waterways from Canton to Yingkow, from Shanghai to Chungking, who made rebellions and quelled them. At once despotic and benign, these men were always splendid in stiff uniform on the bridge, often bedraggled in some waterfront bar — men of all nations who skippered the rusty steamers, the gleaming motorships, the graceful yachts. Up and down the Pearl they went. The Yuan You, the Yangtze, from Tientsin in the north to Hainan far to the south were as familiar as the backs of their hands. He told me how a man, any man, with a knowledge of seamanship, an audacious face and twenty-five dollars U.S. in hand could get himself a master's ticket, or at least a mate's. Granted, it may be a spurious one, but that was enough to open countless doors to opportunity. I listened raptly, carefully storing pertinent bits of information. Someday, when I was a little older, a bit brasher, maybe...

The new chief engineer was an American. He came shuffling aboard one morning while the ship was in drydock. He was old, white haired, tall, thin and, as is often the case with tall, thin men, slightly stooped. His name was Davis. He had never been to sea, had no license, but was an excellent mechanic. It would work nicely, the skipper said. Mr. Davis was a good mechanic but knew nothing of marine engines. I was not a mechanic but I had become a fair operating engineer.

Two days in drydock sufficed, but they were hectic days for engine room and deck personnel alike. We were glad when the yacht was once again at anchor. She looked very smart in her new dress -- the gleaming hull, graceful and white as the breast of a swan, the bright green boot-topping, the glistening, ocher-colored stack, the newly-painted shrouds, the golden figure head, the varnished bulwarks. The water tanks had two fresh coats of cement and were full of sparkling

Manila water. Mice, cockroaches, ants, bedbugs, and snakes had succumbed to the deadly fumes of cyanide disks.

Scarcely a day passed without a visit from the girls of the Baptist Dormitory, to whom the presence of the yacht was doubtless a welcome diversion. They were charming and friendly but incredibly plain of face owing perhaps, to the fact that they were entirely devoid of makeup, with the exception of talcum powder, which they used sparingly. Despite this lack of rouge or lipstick, or maybe because of it, they were quite attractive. They wore their long hair in a tight bun at the nape. Their dresses, too, were long but sometimes quite frilly. They invariably wore high or medium-high heeled shoes and often carried Bibles. They never laughed at even mildly off-color jests, rarely held a boy's hand, certainly never publicly, and were always chaperoned. Their beliefs included not reading the newspaper on Sunday. Visiting hours at the dormitory were strictly observed and held to a minimum. The girls were anything but a sailor's dream, in fact they were quite the opposite. Still, the association with them was pleasant in a way, particularly with those who were less inclined to shyness.

But even they were flustered when I, upon being served a glass of punch at one of their social gatherings in the courtyard of the seminary, innocently expressed the opinion that on so warm a night a glass of cold beer, rather than the sweet punch, would be vastly better. The shapely young woman filling my glass was visibly taken aback. There was much whispering among the girls, and thereafter I sensed a temporary cooling in their demeanor. But this aloofness lasted only a short time, for how can you win a man to Christ if you ostracize him? A very sensible theory indeed, although I thought in my case it failed. But because of them I went to church, and because of them, I readily admit, I had little contact with the baser elements that the seaman usually seeks out in a port.

The Caros, my foster parents, became concerned lest I yield to pressure from the Baptists. Their fondest hope was that I would enter the fold of the Roman Church. I set their minds at ease. I had no intention of joining either church.

Toward the middle of October there was a renewed drive to spruce the ship up. The reason was soon revealed. The captain's family was joining him and, for a part of the next voyage at least, would live on board. We received the news with no little dismay, for not only would we have a woman and children, the bane of all seamen, but with their coming,

Captain and Mrs. Skolfield with their two sons and two of their house staff. This was taken January 28, 1934. From the author's collection.

our freedom would end. No more could we strip and dive into the clear, warm sea on the spur of the moment. Even the skipper agreed, with an understanding grin. And there would be no more boisterous night sessions of singing and arguing, not with children in bed by nine o'clock.

A week before departure, Mrs. Skolfield, a short, heavy woman, came on board, preceded by a couple of very noisy boys of four and seven. The captain called the crew together, introduced his family, then herded them to his stateroom.

We began the second voyage on the twenty-third of October. In the almost fourteen months I had been aboard, I learned much, not only in the engineering profession, but even more so in matters religious. Of the first I originally had little, very little, knowledge; the latter was all news to me. But, as I have said, the well-learned Scripture verses did not find their way to my heart. Consequently, at the start of my second voyage aboard the *Good Tidings*, I had not even considered what I heard in a hundred sermons. Indeed, I had some violent fits of rebellion against what I considered encroachment on my thoughts and private life. I skipped devotions when I could, on occasion going to the extreme of volunteering to clean the bilges, a foul chore I detested. But the rebellion was short-lived, and soon I again recited the Bible verses with the rest of my shipmates. It wasn't too difficult to turn a deaf ear to the skipper's occasional man-to-man talks. When I was told his wife was an accomplished teacher of the Bible, I faced the coming months with trepidation.

19

The Leper Colony

We sailed somewhat abruptly, our departure hastened by an approaching late-season typhoon. Manila harbor is a poor place to weather a storm. The captain had no intention of adding the yacht to the dozen shipwrecks already lining the breakwater the length of the Luneta and Dewey Boulevard, victims of a vicious August typhoon. By sailing at once, he hoped to be out of the storm track the following day. With luck, we would be a hundred-fifty miles to the south, off the Mindoro Coast, when the typhoon hit Manila.

It was a calculated risk, and we lost. Even before we cleared the Bay, the yacht was doggedly fighting a rising sea under an ominous sky. My watch over, I made a quick tour of the ship. Everything was secured for heavy weather including the captain's two boys, who were lashed to chairs. The chairs, in turn, were lashed to the wheelhouse. Mrs. Skolfield was below, beset by the demons of seasickness and diabetes. Holding on to a stanchion, I viewed the grim scene. Overhead, low-flying scud whipped by like tattered, soiled linen. Far to the west, like a glimpse into another, more pleasant world, a patch of sunlit blue stood out boldly, but in a moment that, too, was gone. Only grayness remained, grayness above and on the water below. Sea and sky merged to become one, without form, yet having many forms. Nothing remained of the beauty and serenity of the southern sea; there was only drabness and violence. Twice a minute, the golden figurehead on the sweeping bow disappeared in a welter of foam only to rise, moments later, as if trying to take flight, leaving a trail of white water cascading from the long bowsprit. A steady stream of water spouted from the scuppers, which had barely time to clear the flooded decks before another wave thundered aboard, sucking, clutching, tearing. The wind vane on the mainmast veered crazily as if in the grip of a destructive child, then was wrenched from its seat and hurled into the wild sea. Now and then a squall bore down on our struggling ship, engulfing it in a solid wall of water, choking and strangling.

Yet, as I watched, I couldn't help but admire the extraordinary grace with which the yacht met each sea. If she had wings she'd fly, I thought at one particular moment as the ship swooped up the long slope of a wave and poised briefly on the crest, before plunging into the seething trough.

It was becoming increasingly evident that the typhoon, instead of continuing its northeast sweep, had straightened and was boring almost due west, a not uncommon occurrence in late season. And we were directly in its path. The day was coming to a close and our position was far from comfortable — an approaching typhoon, a lee shore, and night coming on.

Rather than be caught by the typhoon while crossing the Verde Island Passage, the skipper decided to run for shelter in a nearby cove. It was a wise choice for Verde Island passage was rough even in good weather. Entering the sanctuary with the last feeble light of day, we were booted through the narrow, rock-lined inlet by the steep waves and slipped into the calm water, anchoring in the center of the small cove. Almost at once, it seemed, the light was gone, the darkness relieved only by a few yellow lights ashore, and presently even those went out.

Toward midnight the wind, which gradually shifted around the quadrant, increased perceptibly, flinging itself through the night with the rush and wailing of a thousand banshees, and even in the sheltered anchorage, the yacht strained at her chains. Shortly before 1 a.m. the gale abated, and suddenly it was still. The eye of the typhoon hovered over us. Except for the feeble glow from the binnacle, blackness enveloped the bridge, a blackness so intense that at a distance of less than a dozen feet from the compass one lost all sense of direction. For an instant, as we watched, the clouds were torn apart, and a few lavender stars gleamed eerily through the fathomless space; then even they were extinguished. With the coming of the center had come silence, deep, oppressive silence broken only by the distant booming of the surf outside the cove. Occasionally, the still air stirred uneasily, as if some minor demons were flitting about, gathering for the final battle, and now and then one brushed our cheeks with a ghostly kiss and fluttered on. High up, a sighing sound quivered briefly, like the keening of a restless soul, and was gone.

Suddenly a hollow moaning announced the imminent onslaught and almost simultaneously a vicious gust struck the ship. Like a beast at bay, she swung to meet the attack. Then it came. Shrieking and screaming it descended on us. The tortured air howled in agony and the cove, almost landlocked though it was, became a cauldron of nightmarish fury. A sudden tremor ran through the ship as a weakened link in one of the chains gave way under the strain. The rain, driven horizontally by the blast, stung like needles and only the skipper and the mate remained on the bridge wing, shapeless blobs hunched against the gale, staring into the void.

As the fury of the wind increased, the ship, bereft of one anchor, began drifting. The engine room telegraph clanged loudly. Slow speed ahead at first, then half; finally, with the phosphorescent breakers leering eerily from the dark, full, emergency speed. Hour after hour the cyclonic winds roared until, with the coming of a dismal dawn, the violence subsided. By midday it was quiet, with a steady downpour, warm and soothing in its monotony, blanketing the ravaged land.

The wounds of nature, like those of man, heal swiftly. When we left the cove, two days later, the newly laundered land drowsed peacefully behind us, while the blue sea glittered in the noonday sun.

Ellis, the older of the two boys and named after his father, lost little time in getting into everyone's hair. We alternately expected him to sprout wings or horns, so pleasant and mischievous was he by turn. David, only half his brother's age, was no problem, aside from his somewhat frequent fits of screaming during the night.

Concerning the always-smiling Mrs. Skolfield, my worst fears were quickly realized. The day after the typhoon, the captain informed us, during the morning devotions, that henceforth, and here his face broke into a grin, his wife would hold daily Bible classes.

Daily!

I shuddered inwardly and determined that I would somehow find a chore to do in the engine room between 3 and 4 p.m. While not required, it seemed attendance at the classes was expected. Twice a week I didn't mind. But daily...

As if the typhoon had knocked the breath out of the land and sea, a great calm prevailed for two full days and nights after the storm's passage. Even the Verde Island Passage was unusually quiet. But when we ran past cloud-capped Mount Calavite, on the northern end of Mindoro, during the night, the first sharp puffs of the awakening Northeast Monsoon were raising whitecaps. And when we left the Bay of Mamburao the following noon, after a hasty visit ashore, the wind had risen to moderate gale force.

Clear of the land, the sails were hoisted, the engine stopped, and we sped along, silently and smoothly, with a sharp list to port under the pressure of the billowing canvas. It was an incredibly lovely voyage, that run down the Mindoro coast. To our left, the mountainous island stretched as far as the eye could see, lush, dark-green forests alternating with golden, palm fringed beaches or massive promontories. Above us arched the deep blue vault of heaven, dotted with serenely drifting clouds. On our right lay the gently heaving, white-cap-garnished azure South China Sea. And below us gurgled the sparkling, crystal-clear water. How wonderful it was to be alive, to feast the eye on the magnificent face and form of Mother Nature, to draw slow, deep breaths of salty air, to listen to the soft whoosh of the bow wave, and the plaintive mewing of a solitary gull. I glanced at the sun, then tried to visualize the sparkling scene without the golden light — dark, void, barren, and could only agree with my father's oft-uttered opinion that if one had to have a god, it might as well be the sun, without whose benign rays there would be no life. I gave the beautiful world a final loving look, then descended to the quiet engine room to finish the painting I started the day before.

Mr. Davis was standing behind the engine. His head was bent sideways at an alarming angle, and he scowled at an unpainted area between the engine and the big silencer. Turning to me he inquired softly whether I had not forgotten to paint between engine and silencer. My cocky answer turned his face livid. He pointed a trembling hand to the paint bucket, and while I was smearing the paint on, he found his voice. His words were many and colorful, centering around the fact that where there was room for a brush, there was also room for paint, even if the place was out of sight, as I foolishly said.

As we neared the island of Culion, once more under engine power, a copper cooling water pipe sprung a leak. Unable to repair the break satisfactorily with our limited equipment, it was decided to have the pipe brazed in the machine shop of the leper colony. Mr. Davis flatly refused to enter the colony, yet insisted that the repair be made before we left. I wasn't anxious to go either, despite the Reverend Mr. Jansen's assurances the previous year. But the chief had both age and rank, and an hour after our arrival, I stood before the closed gate to the colony, clutching the tube in one perspiring hand, and the permit in the other.

The sun shone as brightly on one side of the fence as on the other; the ground felt and looked the same, and I was certain that the air hadn't changed. Yet, the instant the gate closed behind me, a pall of gloom seemed to fall. The force of gravity surely doubled, for I could barely lift my feet; and for a full minute my lungs absolutely refused to draw in the terrible air. But the tube in my hand reminded me that I had to move on, and my lungs, after a few necessary but tentative and fearful gasps began to function normally. As I strode toward the machine shop, my anxiety was further eased at the sight of the lysol-filled basins along the way. I met a few men and women, but they seemed only mildly afflicted, for I saw no sign of the dread disease. They nodded a cheery greeting and walked on. But approaching the shop, I saw an old man shuffling along the tarred path. Upon seeing me, he stopped, covered his face with gnarled hands and turned away, lest I be sickened by the loathsome sight. I felt a lump form in my throat at such humility.

The mechanic brazed my pipe quickly and skillfully, but I hardly noticed it. Although I tried not to stare at it too fixedly, my eyes were glued to the deep, bubbling hole where his nose once was. When he was done, he grinned at me and pointed to a nearby basin. "Better wash," he said and gave me a slow wink. I daresay, no object ever received so thorough a washing as did my cooling water pipe. And my hands have not been as clean or sterile since, for every basin on the way to the gate added its quota of disinfectant to my pipe and hands.

As we made our slow way down the Palawan Coast, it wasn't long before the vermin once again struggled for supremacy. Only by a concentrated effort at extermination and cleanliness were we able to keep ahead of cockroach, bedbug, centipede and scorpion. Leftover food, soiled clothes and damp shoes were quickly invaded, and every dim corner became a spawning place for the filthy creatures. The roaches seemed to have a particular fondness for the chief engineer, whose protests and complaints became more pointed every day. One morning I saw him standing in the sunlight outside the messroom, intently studying a wriggling cockroach through his bifocals. He had the insect clamped between the jaws of a pair of pliers and was in the process of trying to open its mouth with a toothpick. His efforts were unsuccessful, and finally, his dentures clacking angrily, he flung the insect overboard. In response to my amused question, he muttered, "just wanted to see if he had teeth." He kicked off his left slipper and showed his foot. The tip of his greasy sock had been chewed away. The big toe showed tiny scratches and dried blood. Preceding me below, he explained that he always slept with his socks on and was awakened several times by a pain in his toe. In his cabin he showed me several pairs of dirty socks, all holed, and always at the big toe. He did not seem to think much of my theory that vermin loves nothing better than unclean bodies or clothes, but his socks looked a bit less greasy after that.

There was a slight increase in baptismal rites on our second pass through the islands. But only too often the little knots of new believers who clutched their Bibles as they bade us farewell the previous year fell apart. As we dimmed in their memories, the once-eager converts reverted to Catholicism or paganism, depending on the particular religious abbeys from which they came.

The baptismal rite was the one facet of our mission that I never grew weary of watching. Baptisms were always performed in the presence of as many witnesses as possible, since one reason for the act is the public confession of Jesus Christ. As most of the evangelizing was done among the coast dwellers, the beach was the logical place for the rite, but any river or creek deep enough for immersion, and not too swift, was acceptable, as were lakes or pools. The pools were not popular, however, because being frequently fed by springs, they were too cold. Often there was little change in the faces of the baptized ones. If the saying that the eyes are the windows of the soul is true, then it would seem that the change in the soul should be significant, too. But here and there, and more often as more time was allotted to fully acquaint the people with the scriptural teaching, a radiant man or woman, often young, strong, comely, or sometimes old, feeble, and ugly, would reverently fold the hands, then rise, dripping and gasping, but more radiant still. It was after such baptisms that the skipper invariably took me aside to ask quietly whether it were not time to "follow the Lord's command." And, as invariably, I shook my head, usually quietly, but sometimes vehemently. He always nodded, patted my shoulder, and turned away.

We anchored off the splendidly-curved beach of Cuyo a few days before Christmas. As before, there were a few bad minutes as I watched the sun disappear below the rim of the world on the evening before the holiday. But the homesickness was much milder, for all sorrows and longings ease with the passage of time. I swallowed the lump in my throat and turned my attention to a shore visit that night.

Each house, I noticed, as I walked slowly along the sandy streets, was adorned as festively as the owner's purse permitted. Some were wreathed in multi-colored lights, for the town had a power plant of sorts; others were palely illuminated by a candlelit bamboo-and-tissue-paper star. There were no radios, but now and then the quavering tune of a carol rose from some hidden gramophone. Below one small hut on a side street, two barefoot young men clad in rolled up trousers and white *barongs* were strumming softly on their guitars. Presently they broke into a slow, plaintive song, their eyes lifted to the single, wide window above which hung a huge, blue star. The instant the song started, two mop-haired youngsters appeared in the window and stared at the serenaders for a moment, then ducked back into the room. After a minute or two, a young woman approached the window and halted, barely visible a few feet inside the darkness of the room. Then she came to the window, rested her elbows on the wide sill and cradled her face in her hands. Thus she remained, motionless and in seeming rapt attention, while the troubadours, with scarcely a pause swung into one song after another, all in the same slow, sad tempo, until, in the middle of "La Paloma," she abruptly withdrew, bringing the concert to an end. I walked on, profoundly stirred, not only by the romantic scene, but by the magic of the warm scented night as well.

The serenaders still sing beneath bougainvillea-framed windows on peaceful, fragrant nights in the islands. But they are fewer now, and soon they, too, like all things simple and pleasant, worthwhile things and lovely, will be only a memory as the raucous voice of the radio penetrates to the most isolated barrio. Perhaps even now, from the window where once stood a comely lass listening raptly to the songs of the earnest swains below, squats an ugly, plastic box, flinging its strident tones into the tranquil night under the stately coconut palms, as her suitor calls out from below.

A church had been built since our first visit, a little church of hard-packed dirt, bamboo rafters and nipa thatch. It looked insignificant, almost absurd, in comparison with the massive Catholic Church nearby with its yard-thick walls and solid, iron-fettered doors, its lofty sanctuary and deep-throated bells.

On an impulse, I offered to paint a sign for the humble church. A couple of days later it was finished, with the letters CUYO BAPTIST CHURCH in blue on a background of pure white, and a picture of the Bible superimposed on the golden rays of the sun. The sign was a bit short and too high, but the colors were bright and for a time the sign lent a bit of dash to the drab facade of the little church and, indeed, to the entire street corner. I was pleased.

20

Aground

A day's run brought us again to the southern Palawan coast. As we touched at the countless villages of that island, I found myself going ashore more frequently in search of excitement. Wherever I went at whatever hour, peace and monotony reigned supreme. Life was becoming boring. The first feelings of resentment subconsciously stirred toward the indolent tropical life I led.

Many of our expeditions into the countryside were in search of fresh fruit. The size and richness of the various fruits were a constant source of wonder to me. Who would have thought the cashew nut was but the seed of a much larger yellow-red fruit that was both succulent and sweet? Who would have thought that the malodorous durian could be so tasty and wholesome? Other, better known fruits seemed to grow everywhere, all reaching prodigious size in the warm climate and fertile soil; plump, juicy mangoes, creamy avocados, sweet papayas; all the size of small melons. And for thirst no beverage under the sun equals the cool flavored water in a young coconut.

I spent hours watching the making of copra. At first I followed the cutters from tree to tree as they brought down the brown nuts with long, knife-tipped bamboos. Later I squatted by pile after pile of nuts, watching as they were impaled on pointed shafts set into the ground, the thick husks being twisted off in one swift movement. I marveled at the skill with which the nuts were split, at how deftly the meat was pried from the shell. I gasped and coughed in the smoke of crude kilns in which coconut meat was dried, or breathed deeply the candy-like fragrance of that same meat drying on mats in the hot sun. Occasionally I gagged on the rancid smell of overripe copra. I spent hours admiring the agility of tuba gatherers as, with a short, thick bamboo slung on their backs, they sure-footedly climbed the tall coconut trees to tap the sap at the crown. I sampled the fresh, sweet tuba and

later found the same juice, a few days old, packed a wallop and made me sick.

I visited many people during those boring days, spending many a hot, muggy evening in the small, oil lamp illuminated hut of some girl who caught my fancy, or of some young man who took me home to show off a white visitor. In consequence, I became acquainted with many of the superstitions and tribal laws held sacred by these natives. I was no stranger to superstition, being reared in a house at the edge of a great German forest where fairies, dwarves, and witches dwelt, and where a broken mirror was treated with fear and apprehension. Thus, when a native said that if a girl sang before the stove she would marry an old widower, I found no fault with the belief. If a hen cackled at midnight I was told it meant an unmarried woman had given birth. Similarly, it stood quite to reason that if a pregnant woman cut her hair, her baby would be born hairless. And if I ever dreamed of teeth falling out, I could be assured of a death in my family.

The chief engineer, never overly friendly, became increasingly cantankerous as the weeks passed. Often he took his ire out on me, not always without reason. He never lost his fear of the engine order telegraph. At the first shrill ring, he froze, panic draining the blood from his face. Then he either acknowledged the command, forgetting the maneuver, or leaped to the throttle and forgot to answer. The latter was, of course was not nearly as bad as the former. This was demonstrated graphically one bright morning as we approached the western fringe of the Sulu Archipelago. With the coming of day, the offshore wind died. The surface of the sea was like a burnished, silvery mirror as it reflected the glare of the sun. I sat on the starboard rail, replacing the faulty switch of the running light above me. Overhead, I heard the measured steps of the skipper as he paced back and forth, squinting into the glare of sun and sea. With the sun astern, objects, particularly reefs, show plainly, but the keenest eye cannot pierce the glittering surface of the water, with the sun low and ahead. Looking down, I marveled at how clear the water was, as my eyes followed a long stretch of coral. Because I wasn't facing forward, it was clearly visible. We seemed to fly in crystal pure air over a multi-hued terrain. A large squid, pulsing lazily along, suddenly emitted an inky jet and was gone; a manta ray, lying on a sandy shelf, swooped upward and away, leaving a flurry of settling sand. A school of small, brightly colored fishes made a frantic dash for a clump of white coral. Yes, how clear the deep water was. Or was it so deep...?

At that moment I heard the jingle of the engine room telegraph and the instant acknowledgement. But the diesel pounded on at full speed. Once more the telegraph, high pitched with urgency, shrilled. After a long moment, the engine slowed, then rumbled in reverse. But it was too late. A soft scraping rippled through the ship, stopped, repeated itself, and became a grinding roar as the deadly coral raked the hull. For an instant, the noise ceased; then came a jarring blow as a hundred fifty tons of steel and wood, still traveling at almost cruising speed, rode up a steep ledge and came to an abrupt stop, the jib boom vibrating high over the calm sea. An image of the masts splintering flashed through my brain. I braced myself against the deckhouse. But their stout stays held and the tall masts remained standing.

Hastily taken soundings revealed no leaks. But when we climbed over the side at low tide a few hours later and waded around the stranded ship, we saw how perilously close we had come to disaster. Only inches away on the port bow, a bare yard off the starboard side, and one foot directly ahead, were three huge black rocks thrusting through the sharp coral. A light puff of air from the south, an ever-so-gentle current from the north, or a fraction of a knot more speed, and the yacht's mission would have ended in the twinkling of an eye. As Captain Skolfield later pointed out, it was as if the Hand of

God steered the ship between the rocks and stopped it. He compared it to a child guiding a toy boat among the rocks of a shallow creek.

Fittingly, the captain's devotional text the next morning was "The Power of God." He was more eloquent than usual, dwelling at some length on the incredible pressures locked in a volcano, on the whirling forces of a typhoon, the searing heat in a lightning bolt, the power of the waves, the inexorable rise and fall of the tides. He reminded us of the near-disaster we experienced, and of the power in the Hand that steered us between those massive rocks, and the lesson behind it all. Subtly then, in a lowered voice, he spoke of another power more awesome even than the brute forces unleashed by nature, a power that delved into the hearts and minds of man, a power that could lift a man from the gutter and restore his dignity and usefulness; a power that brought life to the dead, that could snatch a soul from the gates of hell itself; a power pitted against the forces of evil, of darkness, against Satan himself. He spoke of Jesus Christ, who, on the cross refused to employ the mighty forces at his disposal, and elected to die, laden with the sins of the world, so that we, and here the captain paused, his eyes making a slow circuit of our faces, might have life throughout eternity.

For once I walked slowly from the devotions, impressed both at the way the accident turned out and the message.

While waiting for the tide's inexorable drop and rise, the skipper made observations, took bearings and drew thin lines on the area chart. According to these, the yacht should have cleared the vast reef extending 1.4 miles from the gently curving beach of a small island, by almost a mile. Yet the ship had run aground 2.3 miles from the beach in water that showed a deep ten fathoms on the chart. A new reef, thrown up by the frequent earthquakes that ripple the region? Or, an existing reef, mischarted? We never found out.

The Islands of the Sulu Sea

Aside from a few torn copper sheets, the hull was intact. At high tide it was a simple matter to heave the ship off the crushed coral and into the deep water astern. Fearful of other reefs, we anchored during the remaining hours of darkness.

If I live a hundred years, I'll never forget the beauty of that night. Unable to sleep, I went on deck toward daybreak. At first I saw nothing. Then, slowly, bit by bit, the glorious night unfolded before my rapt gaze. The yacht lay motionless on the tranquil sea under a black, glittering sky. Low in the east, Venus heralded the day. Almost overhead, the Southern Cross flamed in blue-white splendor. Farther down curved the ghostly-white arch of the Milky Way, the mysterious flow of the Magellanic Cloud. No sound, not even the whisper of the water, marred the unearthly silence of the deep. The boundary between sea and sky was gone; the two were one, merged into a vast, shimmering vault, breath taking, infinitely lovely. The ship, seeming to cast off the bounds of Earth, floated in the depths of space, coasting silently among the constellations.

A strange mixture of awe and fear came over me, a sudden almost overpowering desire to worship the dread presence that seemed to permeate the glorious night. I felt as if I were at the moment when time ceases and eternity begins. So compelling was the illusion, so terrible, and so real my apprehension, that I shivered despite the warmth. My glimpse into eons yet to come lasted only a short while. Faint, pink fluorescence quivered briefly in the east, steadied, slowly permeated the starry vault, broadened and brightened perceptibly. Soon the passing of time filled the sky with wondrous light and the dawn of a new day.

21

The Moro Princess

For a week we threaded our way among some of the world's most enchanting islands. Their names lay sweetly on my tongue as, time and again I trailed my fingers across the charts and slowly pronounced their names: Pangaturang, Panducan, Datubato, Tubalubac. The ennui which gripped most of us evaporated with the change in scenery. We all felt a keen anticipation at the prospect of another visit to the Sulu Archipelago, with its tranquil waters and lush isles, its lurid tales of piracy and smuggling, its hadjiis and harems, its slender, wavy krises and heavy *kampongs*, its ancient brass *lantakas* and purple pearls.

Our evangelists accomplished little among the natives, who remained content to continue with their Muhammedan or Catholic teachings. But, as everywhere, here and there a toothless oldster, a betel-chewing crone, or a chubby youngster succumbed to the combination of medicine and Gospel, going away healed, we hoped, both in body and spirit.

I often wondered why the Mission was so willing to spend time, money and effort on such seemingly futile voyages. Unlike our first circumnavigation of the southern islands, however, this second voyage showed some hope for success. On the earlier trip we preached and sailed leaving no one to continue the mission. On our second voyage we deposited evangelists at strategic places from which they could keep in touch with the new Christians and help them with their questions and doubts.

Anchoring in the quiet water of Jolo harbor at sunset, we were immediately surrounded by a fleet of bumboats whose loud-voiced occupants sold everything from dried squid to pearls. A few boats drifted slowly by themselves. Their female occupants, bedecked with shimmering rings, bracelets, armbands and anklets, reclined on sunbleached wooden slats behind small, thatched cabins. They approached only after nightfall, calling softly and enticingly from the dark.

The following day Mrs. Skolfield and the children sailed on the weekly steamer for Manila. They planned to meet the yacht at Cuyo six weeks later. We heaved a collective sigh of relief. The Christians on board, as well as those who were not, were happy to be free of her oppressive presence. It wasn't that she was disliked, but the mere fact of her presence curtailed our liberties and, in the case of we non-Christians, our choice of words and worldly desires.

For my part, I looked forward to renewing my acquaintance with the gentle, demure Maimunah, and the vivacious Amy. Thus, when the two girls, accompanied by the more serious Jahara, boarded the yacht one afternoon soon after our arrival, my heart beat high. More than half a year had passed since our meeting, and the two girls, each in a different way, looked more desirable than ever. Amy, it seemed, shuttled back and forth between her homes in Bongao, Tubigindangan, and Jolo during school vacations. Both Maimunah and her sister lived in Jolo.

There followed one exciting day after another, as we lay at anchor just off the Chinese pier. Our teams, in cooperation with the Alliance missionaries, Landis and Gulbranson, ranged the island. With little to do on board, I entertained the girls. Despite Mr. Davis' obvious disapproval but with the skipper's wholehearted permission, I took them swimming, picnicking, and for long walks. I found myself drawn more and more to the two younger ones. So evident had my interest in the girls become that there was talk in the crew's quarters about an impending wedding. My reaction to this brought about a lot of teasing. At nineteen, I had rarely thought of marriage, but when I did, the specter of Islam rose before my eyes. Even so, there were more and more times when that seemed of little consequence. The presence of those two delightful girls was bewitching. A man, I told myself occasionally, could do worse than settle in that bit of Eden. I had seen enough of it to like what I saw.

In the second week of our stay, the captain, the chief engineer and I received an invitation from the *Dayang-dayang*, the real ruler of Sulu, and from her consort, to a luncheon in their country house some distance from the town. The skipper and I accepted readily. Mr. Davis declined, refusing to have anything to do "with those heathens." I thought this strange, because he, not being a Christian, was, by ordinary definition, a heathen himself, although I doubt that he would have agreed to that sort of logic.

Stepping ashore the following morning, I received a pleasant jolt, for by the side of the high, black car on the wharf, stood the three girls. Amy, bubbling over with energy and joy, took my hand and pulled me next to her on the front seat. Maimunah, her soft eyes bright, entered the rear of the car with her sister. Captain Skolfield seated himself between the princess and her husband, the *datu*. We rolled through the town and into the country. Amy kept up a running commentary on the sights and smells, as we sped along the narrow, dusty road.

The house was a rambling affair of wood and thatch, raised off the ground by massive hardwood posts. A wide stairway led to a veranda that surrounded the upper level. The windows were high. The gentle breeze wafting through the rooms billowed the lacy curtains inward on one side and outward on the other. The house looked solid but old and in need of paint. The dining room was large, lofty and dark because of the paneling which was a reddish-brown color. A huge table stood in the center laden with food, and ringed by benches. Little alcoves were cut into the walls, each with a single, oversized cushion.

A light-skinned young woman of perhaps twenty-five was reclining on one of the cushions. A little girl played nearby. The woman rose at our entrance. She was small and slender but regal of carriage and, while not exactly beautiful, possessed a wholesome comeliness which even her filed teeth and tightly combed hair could not erase. This was the princess Tarhata, formerly a student at the University of Illinois. Upon the death of Sultan Kiram of Sulu she left the University, hurrying home to assist in the rule, within the Commonwealth, of the far-flung islands of the Sulu Sea. This I learned quickly in a few seconds from the lovely, talkative Amy.

We were quickly seated, the skipper between the *Dayang-dayang* and Tarhata. Near the head of the table sat *Datu* Ombra, the consort, while at the other end were Jahara and the little girl. I was between Maimunah and Amy on the right side. I had never seen royalty, so I gave the two princesses my undivided attention and tried not to appear too awed.

The *Dayang-dayang* was the exact opposite of Tarhata, fat, dark and about twice as old. Her husband was short and chubby, twenty years her junior, and very friendly. In contrast to her husband, who spoke the English language fluently, the *Dayang-dayang* spoke only the local language and a bit of Arabic. What fascinated me most about her was not her ringed fingers, nor the enormous pearl on her ample bosom, but the extra finger on her right hand, growing outward from the little finger.

After the lunch which, thanks to my two bewitching partners, I scarcely tasted, we stretched ourselves on the soft cushions to digest the meal. Only the three girls were absent, having left the room as we settled into the luxurious silk. I wondered what became of them and was getting restless when Amy beckoned to me from the door. She was wearing a bathing suit. Quietly, for the others were dozing, I tiptoed across the room. Maimunah and Jahara, also in bathing suits, were sitting on the stairs. Fortunately, I always wore my swimming trunks under my clothing and a few minutes later we were splashing in the surf not far from the house. It was an unforgettable afternoon — the sparkling day and the warm, blue water, the lively, uninhibited girls. Even demure Maimunah and sober Jahara were soon caught up in the gaiety, and their joking, giggling, and little screams were delightful to hear. But the best was still to come. Weary at last of the boisterous activity, the girls led me to a large, rockbound pool at the near edge of the garden, poised briefly at the pool's rim then plunged into the black water. I followed unsuspectingly and almost drowned. The water, fed by springs was ice cold. When I surfaced, gasping, the little minxes joined forces and pushed me down. Even below the surface I could hear their silvery laughter.

When the skipper appeared an hour later, we were sitting on the rocks, spent but happy. He snapped a few pictures then we walked toward the house. Somehow, I lagged behind with Maimunah and as we walked slowly along the narrow path, a strange sensation came over me. Could it be real, this tranquil scene and this lovely honey-skinned girl by my side? I looked about. A deep silence lay over the garden disturbed only by the singing of birds or the occasional humming of a bee. Vividly-hued flowers gleamed in the dark-green foliage wherever the eye strayed, rioting colors from the palest yellow to the deepest red, flung about as if in wild abandon by a mad painter. Not a petal stirred, not a leaf. And over all hung the scent of a thousand blossoms. The story of Eden was familiar to me, a pleasant fantasy, I thought, born of longing in the mind of some Bedouin in the arid desert. But as I walked on in that solemn silence, breathing the cool, perfumed air, surrounded by every color imaginable, something akin to awe stole over me and suddenly the Garden of Eden was a reality, not the figment of someone's imagination. For a few moments, the Biblical account took on new meaning. Eden must have been thus at the dawn of man. But whatever the feeling was it didn't last. Then I was back in the world, walking along a narrow path, a sweet, silent girl at my side. By a bush, shielded from the house, we halted. I was aware of a vague breathlessness, aware too, of a current that flowed between us, ebbed and flowed yet again, only stronger. A word, I sensed, or a single gesture, and Maimunah would be in my arms. What, then, was the strange wall that seemed to rise between us when the words of love were poised to tumble from my dry lips? Thus we stood, the blond young man from the West and the lovely, golden-skinned girl of the East, wordlessly gazing into each other's eyes.

On the way back to Jolo, it was Maimunah who sat beside me in the high, straight-backed seat. We were passing a large, two-story house which stood a short distance from the road, when Amy asked that the car be stopped. Leaning forward, she pointed to the house and said, "They have a Moro baptism there this afternoon. Would you like to see it?"

I looked at the skipper who, after a short consultation with the *datu*, nodded. We thanked their Royal Highnesses for the lunch and alighted. The car went on and soon disappeared in a cloud of dust. We walked the short distance to town.

That afternoon, at the foot of the polished hardwood stairs, the girl's sandals and our shoes joined the variety of footwear already there. Barefoot, except for the skipper, who wore socks, we entered the building. The room was large but, because of the number of people already assembled and the absence of a breeze, oppressively hot. We seated ourselves close together on the gaudy mats on the floor. It was a very uncomfortable position for both the skipper and I, but quite easy for the girls who simply crossed their feet, hitched their skirts up and let their knees swing outward.

Since it was obviously a "heathen" ceremony, I wondered why the captain decided to come. My thoughts were interrupted by a young woman who entered, dressed in the traditional Moro attire of a very tight, brightly-colored, many-buttoned jacket and long tight skirt. She carried an armful of tall, slender plants, on which about twenty bell-like blossoms grew along the top twelve inches. Distributing the plants among the guests; she then withdrew. Upon receiving the flowers, the guests fell silent. Five minutes passed, while a slight breeze ruffled the curtains at last, mercifully dispelling the heat in the crowded room. Maimunah sat at my right, occasionally sending a shy smile my way. How black were her eyes, how red her full lips. Amy sat next to the captain, smiling brightly at those near her. The blood of your own race flows in their veins, I reminded myself, torn between my budding love for both girls.

The door abruptly opened and a Muslim priest, white-bearded, wizened and small, entered. We rose, folding both hands around the slender stems of our tall flowers, and looked expectantly at the *Imam*. After a solemn pause he opened the black bound Koran in his hands and in a quavering voice began to read, stopping frequently to allow the guests to repeat his words, Although I was ignorant of the language, I strove valiantly to at least <u>sound</u> like one of the crowd. I stole a glance at the skipper. He was silent, but his face was red as he glared at the top of his flower. When the chant ended, we resumed our seats. Presently, another door opened and an old woman, carrying a baby in her arms, entered, followed by an exceedingly self-conscious young couple, the child's parents. The old woman held the child toward the priest. He placed his hands on the infant's head, then, facing toward the sunset, and Mecca, intoned a monotone prayer beginning with the phrase that is heard all around the Muhammedan world morning, noon and evening. "*Lebeika, Allahuma, labbeika! La Illaha Illa Allah! Muhammed Rasulu Allah!*" When he ended, he severed a lock of the sleeping infant's hair and placed it in the lower half of a coconut from which the meat had been removed. The bottom half, I learned later, contained a small amount of aromatic water. The edges of the two sections of the polished nut were serrated so neatly that the upper half fitted perfectly into the lower.

After the customary refreshments were served, chocolate, tea, and sweets, we bade our host farewell. Putting on my tennis shoes at the bottom of the stairs, I looked into the room under the staircase. A young girl of about fourteen was sitting by the window. Her body was covered with a shapeless, sack-like gown of rough texture. Her face was painted stark white, making her black eyes and red lips stand out sharply. An old woman, a book in her lap, sat in front of the girl. Seeing my stare, Maimunah took my hand and pulled me away, explaining that the girl was being prepared for marriage and was even then reciting long portions of the Koran, which she was compelled to memorize. I was struck quite violently by the tragic expression in the girl's dark eyes. There was none of the joy one normally sees in the eyes of a would-be bride, none of the glow and sparkle of love. There was only anguish and resignation. The utter hopelessness in those eyes was heartrending. How did a parent-arranged marriage work out? What were the compensations, or were there any at all? Would the tender young woman in that dark room beneath the stairs be merely a drudge, a servant, someone to mate with, to bear children? I had seen little affection between Moro couples, seldom more than a thin smile, if even that. They appeared to reserve their affection for their offspring who, it seemed, could never do wrong. That the women desired, and were capable of love, I did not doubt. I had seen it, not only in the hopeless sadness of the girl in that room, but in a pair of soft, dark eyes that same day. Did they hope for the miracle of love after the wedding? It would be a long time before I found the answer, given in a whisper: "Sometimes — sometimes love comes later. If it does not come at all, one must learn to go through life without it."

22

A Moro Dance

For two weeks we made our way slowly southward, eastward, westward, touching islands that in those days were on few charts, little isles that were mere sandbars yet held a few houses perched on stilts. Sanitation facilities were non-existent in many cases and health conditions were often appalling. Our medical men kept busy attending the needs of the bodies, while the evangelists strove valiantly to redeem the souls.

There was a never-ending stream of sick, maimed, and sometimes dying. Beri-beri, malaria, tropical ulcers, and festering sores made up the bulk of the complaints. One calm, brilliant morning, a feverish old man was carried on board, his left foot swathed in dirty leaves. I watched as the doctor gingerly unwrapped the leaves, aware of an ever increasing, sickly-sweet odor that polluted the clean air — the terrible smell of gangrene. Fearful, yet fascinated, I looked at the swollen, discolored foot and the huge blob that was once the big toe. The doctor turned to the interpreter.

"It has to come off — now. He'll die if it doesn't."

There followed a short consultation between the interpreter and the man's relatives. Now and then one of the dark-faced men cast a sideways glance at the doctor.

The interpreter turned to the doctor and said softly, "More better you leave him alone, sir."

The doctor's mouth fell open. "He'll be dead by Sunday."

"He will not die if you operate?"

The doctor shrugged. "I can't guarantee that. It's pretty far gone."

"Then you better not touch him, because," the interpreter took a deep breath, "if he dies, you die, too."

The doctor looked angrily at the three husky men grouped around the patient's head; then reached for the hypodermic.

I watched, hypnotized, getting sicker all the time, as the doctor cut off the toe and much of the surrounding area and flung the putrid mess overboard. Abruptly my vision blurred, the sunlight faded, my stomach heaved. I barely made it to my cabin and collapsed on the bunk.

We remained three days although only one was scheduled. By the third day, the patient was sufficiently recovered that his people were convinced he would live.

It was interesting to observe the ever-changing reception we received from island to island, ranging from a friendliness of sorts to outright hostility. Captain Skolfield sought to avoid the latter type of islands as much as possible, for the safety of crew and ship. But it couldn't always be done. In waters so dotted with reefs and shoals and inadequately charted as were the Sulu and Celebes Seas at the times, night navigation was hazardous. With the coming of the night the time-worn phrase "any old port in a storm" became quite real.

Only in our case there were no storms, only darkness and treacherous waters.

Such an "old port," at dusk one day, was one of the hostile islands. An hour before sunset the skipper rang down for slow speed. He wanted to time our approach so it coincided with the islanders' suppertime. Then the danger of being spotted was minimal. There was only one safe anchorage, an almost landlocked little cove on the west side of the island, accessible through a narrow, sandbar-flanked inlet. The hoped-for offshore wind, which would blow the smoke and rumble of our exhaust seaward, did not materialize. Thus, an hour after sunset, and with only the faint zodiacal light to guide him, the skipper pointed the yacht into the darkness of the cove. He ordered the engine stopped even before the ship completely negotiated the inlet, letting her drift to the center of the anchorage. To avoid the loud rattle of the chain, the anchor was paid out link by link until it lay on the bottom. We were instructed to use no light, and speak only in low voices and never to whisper, for whispering is quite audible. Ordinarily, a single guard sufficed to patrol the ship from dusk to dawn. On that night, however, one officer and two men stood two-hour watches. My watch, together with two young seamen, was from eleven to one. My heart was in my throat the entire time, while my imagination ran wild. The sky was bright with countless stars, but around us was the blackness of the jungle, relieved only by a slightly less black gap where the inlet was. Through it I could see the reflections of the stars on the calm sea outside. Occasionally, a throaty cry floated through the night, accentuating the stillness. I stared wide-eyed into the darkness, my sight and hearing sharpened by apprehension. Every hoarse cry ashore signalled a wild man's presence, every splash of fish or crocodile was a paddle in the hands of a killer. Twice I started for the forward bell to sound the alarm. On the bridge, the captain was pacing barefoot. I doubt that he slept at all that night. His occasional soft "on deck" ensured that we remained awake. In my case, he had nothing to fear. I have never been so tense. But the watches came and went, the night passed and fortunately nothing happened. With the pink dawn we were on our way.

Rather than run farther south to Sitankai and then up the dangerous Borneo coast, dodging reefs and shoals on the way to Sandakan for our yearly clearance, the skipper decided to get the Philippine clearance for Borneo in Cagayah Sulu, an island west-northwest of our position. From there we could sail directly to Sandakan in deep water most of the way. We would then re-enter the Philippines at Sitankai and touch the missed islands on the way north in another sweep of Tawi-tawi.

At Cagayah Sulu a German came on board, a Jewish trader, who requested passage to Borneo. He was about twenty-five years old and quite brash. Having found a countryman, he lost no time making himself comfortable in my bunk. Although I seldom slept in the cabin, being more comfortable on a mat spread on the deck, I was somewhat annoyed by his forwardness. But he was of such a good humor, and had so many tales to tell, that I soon became genuinely fond of him. He used my toilet articles freely, grandly exclaiming one morning, as he lathered his beard with my soap, "Ah, what good friends we are! What is yours is mine." I waited for him to complete the phrase, but he merely smiled and reached for my safety razor.

At dinner that day, my new friend asked if I would accompany him to a dance, a Moro dance, the same evening. I nodded. It would be a welcome diversion. When he told me it was somewhere in the hills, I had second thoughts. But in the end I went, although not too eagerly. The jungle was dark and eerie, becoming darker and more alien as we went deeper. Hordes of mosquitoes attacked us, their greedy buzzing the only sound. I wondered how my companion was able to follow the right path, for there were several, dim, gray ribbons barely distinguishable in the moonlight where the jungle was thin, invisible where it grew thick. After trudging for a long time, my friend stopped, scratched his head and confessed that he had no idea where we were. Wonderful. At that instant I spied a feeble yellow light to our right, and a few minutes later we stood before a bamboo fence surrounding a small nipa house. In response to our call, a man appeared at the top of the ladder, descending when he saw us. Fortunately, and surprisingly, he spoke a bit of English. He knew where the dance was and indicated the direction. We thanked him profusely and left. We had gone only a few steps when he called us back and, fixing his eyes on my companion, said, "If you want to leave this dance alive, let our women alone."

With that dire warning, he turned and climbed up the ladder. I was all for returning to the ship at once, but my friend shrugged and walked away. Some ten minutes later, we heard drums, voices, and occasional laughter, and presently we saw the faintly-lighted windows of a house. At the gate I eyed the structure dubiously, wondering how so flimsily constructed a house could possibly hold enough people for a dance. There was no use announcing our presence at the foot of the ladder as is the custom, because we would not have been heard anyway. We simply climbed up and entered.

There was only one fairly large room, in addition to the kitchen. One corner was partitioned off as a store room for mats and pillows. A single kerosene lamp, hanging from a rafter by a wire, shed a feeble glow. The men squatted along one wall, talking and chewing betelnut. Their blood-red streams of saliva weren't always successfully spat through the half inch spaces in the bamboo floor. On the opposite side of the room the women were engaged in similar activities, but speaking more and spitting less. Some didn't chew or talk at all, but sat demurely on the floor, their backs resting against the wall. All the guests wore the traditional Moro garb. The men's costumes included wicked looking krises and daggers, both within easy reach in the broad sashes around their waists. I glanced at my friend who already was squatting between two burly Moros, engaged in conversation. Recalling the warning of the man who gave us directions, I wondered what my trader friend did to merit such a remark. I sincerely hoped he would behave himself.

Finding a space between two younger men, I wedged myself in. After a while the combination of kerosene fumes, sweat and betelnut juice became overpowering and I began to feel somewhat nauseated. Fortunately, at that moment, everyone rose, drawing some of the cooler, less odorous air from beneath the house. The women formed a tight circle in the center of the room, while the men arranged themselves in a larger circle around them. My companion also leaped to his feet and took his place, leaving me squatting, alone and embarrassed, against the wall.

The girls joined hands and began moving in time to the drums, tilting their heads back and casting mischievous glances at the men. They moved in a light but restrained manner because of their tight skirts. As the women moved faster, the men, also clasping hands, started in the opposite direction. The men chanted in unison to which the women replied. It was more like ring-around-a-rosy than a dance. Three steps were made very softly, but the fourth came down with an earthshaking bang, fifty feet pounding as one. Thump-thump-thump-WHUMP. The house shuddered and groaned, and now and then a lizard, dislodged from the ceiling, fell, disappearing between the floor slats.

After watching for a few minutes, the rhythmic beat of the drums worked itself into my feet. I got up, wormed my way between two Moro men, grasped their sweating hands and joined the fun. I had no idea what was being chanted, but a look at the glittering eyes of the girls and the lascivious glances of the men, combined with the sensual beat of the hidden drums, told me plainly that more than mere prancing was in the offing. My friend, aside from an occasionally longing glance at the bosoms of the well-endowed younger women, behaved admirably. There was no break in the dancing which grew faster and more fevered by the minute. The chanting became higher pitched and more intense. Worn out and concerned about the effect on my trader companion, I abruptly pulled free of the clutching hands and stepped from the circle. Tapping my friend on the shoulder as he galloped by, we left.

Two days later, off the coast of North Borneo, our mosquito-laden trek into the wilderness came back to haunt me. I suddenly shivered uncontrollably despite the 110 degree heat in the engine room. I was familiar enough with malaria to recognize the symptoms. When I was relieved from my watch at sunset, instead of eating dinner, I fell into bed and tried to sleep. But the chills came at such a rapid rate and were so violent that I was alarmed and reported to the skipper, who ordered an immediate injection of quinine. For a few hours I experienced torture as the germs, greedily feeding on my red blood cells, reproduced rapidly. I was beset by a fearful headache, convulsive fits and chills that were followed by a burning, dry heat that almost drove me insane. My thirst was insatiable; my head boomed, but worst of all was the hot, prickly fire on my skin. But thanks to the prompt massive doses of quinine, I was up in a short time.

When the chief engineer, in a rare show of friendliness, suggested that we find some entertainment the last evening in Sandakan, I eagerly agreed. I was in a devil-may-care mood which, despite, or because of, my constant exposure to Christianity, seemed to come upon me more and more frequently as if I were unconsciously endeavoring to crowd as much carnal pleasure into my life before... This was where I always stopped thinking and tried to quell the uncomfortable feeling that a change was inevitable, that someday...

23

The Sea Gypsies

We sailed past Balhalla's cliffs as the sun rose, heading south-east for Sitankai. I felt exceedingly well that morning, joyously climbing up and down the shrouds. I didn't know then that my malaria had merely subsided and would, a few months hence, and for years to come, assault me at three day intervals, always at ten o'clock in the morning, leaving me weak and gasping. But of this I was unaware that bright, cool morning, off the Borneo coast, and my heart sang, for we were headed again for the islands of the Sulu Sea.

We approached Sitankai at dusk and saw a marvelous sight. Ahead, less than a mile away, a fleet of hundreds of native boats rode at anchor on the glassy sea, one of the great floating villages of the Bajao Sea Gypsies. The sun dropped into the Borneo jungle behind us. The soft tropic night with its accompanying coolness swiftly fell on island and sea. In the boat village a thousand lights flickered and flitted like fireflies, and over the water there floated the eerie moaning of conch shells mingled with the fast rhythm of numerous gongs. As we drifted slowly past, I saw that the fireflies were torches, carried back and forth by the occupants of the boats. In each vessel a cooking fire glowed in the bow and showers of sparks rose high in the still air as here and there a woman or a child directed a stream of air at the glowing charcoal through a long bamboo tube. Above the moaning of the shells and the beat of the gongs rose the wail of children, the sharp voices of women, and the occasional shout of a man. On one boat, silhouetted by the fire behind her, a woman was rinsing the supper dishes in the sea.

Strangely, the Bajaos, though they live almost exclusively on the water and hastily leave the firm land at the first sign of a storm, are the most wretched of sailors and the poorest of fishermen. They are pagans and have only the vaguest concept of an afterlife. There were no Christian missionaries among them, but the Mohammedans were busy, although with only nominal success.

I was told the sails of the more venturesome and better sailors among the sea gypsies are sometimes seen as far north as Zamboanga and as far south as Celebes and Java, but the main Bajao fleet never ventures more than a few score miles from Sitankai, the rendezvous of the tribe. There the boat villagers can be found at anchor except during the times they follow the fish, much as nomads follow their flocks.

The Bajaos bury their dead, not in the sea, but in huge community graves ashore. When death comes, the family boat is cut up and used as a coffin, a family being allowed only enough room on the burial mound for one grave. With each new death, the bones in the grave are dug up, wrapped in a white sheet and placed on top of the new coffin which is then placed in the original grave and covered with sand. Burial rites are simple. The body is merely washed with the prescribed amount of water: thirty coconut shells for an adult, twenty-five for children, and fifteen for new-born infants.

The 18 mile wide Sibutu Passage, separating Sitankai and Sibutu from the rest of the Tawi-tawi Islands, was quiet, but a few minutes before 4 p.m., as we were approaching the island of Simunul, we suddenly sighted a line of breakers directly ahead. The foaming line rushed at us with appalling speed, growing taller and more tempestuous even as we watched, and in less than five minutes the yacht was all but overwhelmed in a tide-rip, that fearful phenomenon which occurs when two conflicting tides clash. For half an hour the ship tossed and turned and bucked in the whirlpools and wild waves that rose sharp and slender like stalagmites then collapsed only to rise again, frothing, boiling, roaring. Viewing the terrifying spectacle, I found it easy to see how even a sturdy vessel could be literally torn apart under the twisting and wrenching of the currents and swallowed by the seething, sucking maelstroms.

Abruptly, the wild show was over and the tide flowed smoothly once more.

We anchored off the village of Tubindangan that night, aware of the swift current that swept along the coast of the low island. The skipper went ashore the next morning ac companied by the medical team and the evangelists. When they returned, just before sunset, I was astonished to see a white man in a rumpled suit and the laughing girl beside him. Amy! I was even more surprised when Amy and her father made no move to return to the village that night.

After we were under way the following morning, the captain informed me that for the next forty-eight hours my sole duty would be to entertain the lovely Amy. Thus, we cruised slowly among some of the world's most beautiful islands, while the shore parties came and went, while the crew worked and stood watch. And while both the skipper and his guest smiled benignly, I spent the hours with the vivacious young woman, playing shuffleboard, swimming, or just chatting. One youthful sailor, more brash than the rest and perhaps a bit jealous, endeavored to join in a game at the instant that the captain stepped on deck. He lost interest after the skipper took him aside for a few moments.

It was plain enough to me, as to everyone else on board, why I was chosen to entertain the young woman. I didn't mind. Indeed, I was enjoying myself wonderfully, with never a thought of marriage. Not, that is, until the night during which we made one of our infrequent night runs. In late evening, the yacht was slipping smoothly through the dark waters of the Sulu Sea. Her white, red and green running lights glittered like jewels in the clear tropic night as if vying with the brilliance of the southern stars. Now and then, gracefully like a ballerina she lifted her forefoot to the light swell, then gently dipped it again into the warm water. Myriad fluorescent stars leaped to life at the touch, danced and crackled along the hull and merged with the shimmering wake. The decks were silent save for the murmuring exhaust and the whisper of the bow wave. We sat on the broad rail, saying little, enjoying the beauty of the night. A mile or so to port the black silhouette of an island crept slowly by. The light offshore breeze, laden with the fragrance of night blossoms, wafted across the water and over the decks. We inhaled deeply, very much aware of each other. Amy, her face raised to the glittering sky, lifted one hand as if to pluck the stars from their purple tapestry; then the hand fell, and she looked at me. Her eyes were like large, dark pools. I leaned toward her, as if impelled by unseen hands stretched forth from the radiant night. But once again, as in the garden, a subtle yet strangely compelling force made me halt even as my heart yearned for the quiet girl at my side. Glancing sideways I noticed we were clear of the island and the heady fragrance. Only the sea breeze was left, sweeping away the last of the perfume — and the thoughts.

When we parted the next morning, Amy was subdued. Wordlessly, I handed her my autograph album. She thought a moment, then wrote rapidly in the Moro language. Placing the book in my hand, she quickly turned away.

It was a long time before I found someone willing to translate her words. Then a lump formed in my throat and I remembered the radiant night so long ago and so far away.

"I love you very much. Remember that always," she had written.

24

The Hadjii

Leaving Bongao, we headed northeast for South Ubian, a relatively large island on the eastern fringe of Tawi-tawi. After a run of less than a day, we anchored a mile off the beach. A few years earlier the island was a major base for pirates. Even in the 30's it lost none of its unsavory reputation. Although the dreaded Moro pirates no longer operated on their once-grand scale, South Ubian was still a smuggler's base. It appeared to drowse innocently and peacefully enough in the hot sun, but reverted quickly to its former lawlessness with the coming of night. There seemed to be no particular attempt to conceal the illicit traffic, the only concession to secrecy being to wait until nightfall. As a practical matter this simply made their activities more difficult to discover. It was at night that the flotillas came, having stood off, hull-down, during the daylight hours — boats from Java,

The Islands of the Sulu Sea

from Celebes, from nearby Borneo — discharging their contraband cargoes. Completing their unloading in a frenzy of activity, they sailed long before dawn, when the island once more lay serenely innocent on the tranquil sea.

Although I knew none of this that sunny morning, I sensed that all might not be well when I heard the captain's orders. Leaving the ship with the medical and evangelical teams, he instructed us to shorten the anchor chain, have the engine on stand-by, and keep a sharp lookout. We watched the boat, oars glinting in the morning sun, approach the beach, ground, and disembark the men. One man remained tying the boat to an oar driven into the sand a few yards above the tideline. Appropriately it was the same method used by old-time pirates, who frequently had to get away in a hurry. In another minute, the party disappeared in the gloom of a coconut grove where the village was.

Our few tasks completed shortly before noon, we were lounging on deck when our attention was drawn to a movement between us and the island. It was our longboat, cleaving the water under the pressure of frantically flashing oars. The skipper stood in the bow, waving his arms wildly and shouting. Although we couldn't understand his words, we suspected something was wrong. Scattering quickly, the bosun and seamen manned the anchor winch, we engineers went below, the mate and quartermaster manned the bridge. A few minutes later the yacht churned her way seaward in a long sweeping curve, the boat still hanging in the davits.

Then Captain Skolfield told the story. On reaching the village, he contacted the head man and requested directions to the barracks of the Constabulary, a garrison of seven enlisted men and one officer. The chief personally conducted our team to the cemetery, where he pointed to eight graves. The soldiers were slain, the chief insisted, because of their arrogance and cruelty. More likely the skipper told us, because they were putting a crimp into the smuggling business.

As was his custom, the captain then asked the chief's permission to treat the sick and wounded. This was readily granted, and a make-shift clinic set up in the village square. There were the usual grins and grimaces, the usual banter and giggling as festering sores were cleaned, boils lanced, knife wounds sewn together, ulcers scraped, teeth pulled, and eyes washed. Then one burly fellow, upon receiving an injection, collapsed in a faint. Instantly the banter, the giggling ceased. Eyes darkened, and here and there the word "murder" fell from betelnut stained lips even as restless fingers curled and uncurled about the hilts of dagger and kris. As calmly as they could our men dumped their medicines and equipment into their bags and retreated, slowly at first, with some pretense at dignity, then headlong, the sullen crowd at their heels. Not waiting for the guard in the boat to extract the oar from the sand, they plunged into the water and most ignominiously clambered aboard.

There was a happy sequel to the story, however. Some time later, on another island, the skipper came face to face with the man he "murdered." The Moro, all smiles and full of apologies, had recovered and begged the captain to pay another visit to the island of South Ubian.

It was in Tawi-tawi that I met the owner and master of a harem. He came aboard one afternoon, a white-haired, white-bearded, short Muslim wearing a white robe, with sandals on his bare feet. His face was the color and texture of leather, but the black eyes were young and twinkling as he conversed in halting English with the captain. I stood nearby, eyes, ears and mouth wide open. His bodyguards, two husky, elderly Moros, remained near the gangway, shuffling their calloused bare feet on the white deck.

Suddenly, a grin on his round face, the skipper asked, "And how many wives have you, Hadjii?"

The old man spread his hands. "Tomorrow I will bring the book. The names are there."

Early the next day he returned, carrying a large, thin, blue-bound, stained book. This he handed to the captain. The names were there, one on each line, with the wedding date next to each name. The fading entries were in a firm, young script. The brighter, later ones became progressively shakier and larger. Beginning in 1876, the most recent entry was 1930. Thirty-six lines. The skipper looked up.

"Thirty-six," he said slowly and shook his head.

The hadjii placed a hand on the skipper's arm and said earnestly, "Thirty-six, yes. But some are and some are not."

Apparently some had died.

The captain turned the pages. More names, thirty to a page and five on the fifth. The hadjii's offspring numbered one hundred-twenty-five children. I was impressed.

Our meandering took longer than anticipated. The time for our rendezvous with the captain's family at Cuyo was long past. Thus, as we tied up at the Jolo pier shortly before noon, we were informed there would be no shore leave. Sailing was set for 4 p.m. when fueling was complete. As the oil and water flowed into their respective tanks, I became increasingly restive, pacing aimlessly, now along the deck, then on the pier, glancing anxiously at the town whence presently, I fervently hoped, a young woman would emerge, a sweet, demure girl, ruby-lipped, with large, soft eyes — Maimunah. Abruptly, as sailing time drew near, a wild longing came over me, and I would gladly have given ten years of my life to swim once more in the cold rockbound pool, listening to the silvery laughter of the three charming girls, to walk one last time in the cool, fragrant garden.

Then I saw her. Wearing the same pink dress she wore when I first met her. She was walking slowly, accompanied by half a dozen other girls. They leaped lightly aboard and were at once surrounded by the eager crew. On seeing the others I experienced a keen disappointment, desiring nothing more than to be alone with Maimunah. I need not have worried. For once taking the lead, she smiled at me, then walked slowly aft. Settling herself in a wicker chair, she waited while I sat on the broad rail. We said little, happy to be together again. We had parted before, and met again, and although I had every intention of returning, I somehow sensed it would be the last time that I gazed at this bewitching young woman. She, too, must have felt it. I saw in her eyes a great regret that matched my own.

The engine room telegraph rang harshly. Maimunah's eyes widened, her full, soft lips parted. Then she stood up. I slid off the rail, and for a long moment we faced each other, as if trying to burn each other's image into our hearts. Neither smiled. Then, her eyes steadfastly on mine, she asked softly.

"Will you ever...forget me?"

I shook my head, unable to trust my voice, and accompanied her to the pier. One last long look, a final, shy wave, and she turned away.

As I sat alone on the stern railing a few days later, watching the sun drop into the Sulu Sea, I considered the immediate future glumly. After the exciting weeks in Tawitawi the prospect of another quarter-year of monotony and

Bible learning along the Palawan coast looked grim indeed. Everything paled in comparison to the delights of the past two months. In tune with my mood, the blood-red sun disappeared behind a filigree of black clouds. I gazed upward. Overhead, the sky was still gold, turning a verdant green toward the east, then cerulean blue. Farther down, the blue deepened, becoming a pale indigo at the edge of night. When my eyes finished their circuit of the heavens, my mind was made up. The mail steamer would touch at Cuyo on her way north. When she sailed, I would be aboard. As often before, I had no idea what I would do when I got to my destination. Take a steamer south and like Wilhelm Schuck settle in Tawi-tawi? A warm welcome awaited me there, and a pair of soft arms. Or should I leave the Philippines entirely? I didn't know, nor did I care.

A sailor who occasionally helped in the engine room took my place. When the steamer, after loading the usual cargo of cattle, copra, and shells, weighed anchor, I was on the short promenade deck. Surprisingly I was only mildly sorry to go. But when we headed north and I gazed southward where, below the rim of the sea, lay the Sulu Islands, a wave of nostalgia washed over me. It brought a feeling of loss that even the charming Cuyo girl who stood at my side could not dispel.

25

Return to Shanghai

The Caros no longer lived in Manila. I took a room with a family I had known for a long time. I was miserable and lonely despite the pleasant company of college student boarders and the landlord's two charming teenage daughters. As the days stretched into a week, then two, I grew restive, wandering aimlessly about the old, narrow streets or spending time in the nearby cinema. I carefully avoided the vicinity of the Baptist Church and the restraining influence of its girls. Indeed I began looking with some interest on the Roman Church, to which my landlord's family belonged. Whether this was because I was extraordinarily fond of Nenita, the youngest daughter of the house, I didn't even try to analyze. When Nenita's father casually pointed out one evening that since one had to have a religion, it only made sense to pick the religion of the land, I hedged but promised to give it serious thought. But before I could fulfill that promise, my course, as often before, changed again. I remembered Shanghai and Mr. Farjoe, the former chief officer of the Gospel Ship. The German steamer *Duisburg* was berthed at Pier Seven. I went on board. "Ja," they needed a messman, and, "ja," I could have the job.

A week later, in early October, I stood once more on Shanghai's *Bund*, shivering, and wondering how to get to Love Lane number seven, the address the mate gave me in one of his letters. A passing rickshaw runner stopped, eyeing me curiously. Yes, he knew where Love Lane was. I climbed aboard, not knowing how far it might be or how much it might cost. Soon we were jogging up broad Bubbling Well Road and passed the huge race track on our left.

Mr. Farjoe was away on a trip, the landlady said, and she had no idea when he would be back. If I wished, I could rent bed space in an attic room. I wished, and soon was seated on a cot in the cold attic, trying to figure out what to do. My money would not last a month, and it was quite clear that I would have to find work or starve, unless Mr. Farjoe returned.

My roommates, eight of them, worked at various trades. I quickly learned the wages were adequate, but they were only able to afford meager quarters because so much money was spent on vice.

I soon found a job, repairing electric heaters in the Soochow Creek plant of the Shanghai Power Company.

Abruptly the relatively mild weather turned cold as the wind veered to the north blowing off the desolate tundras of Siberia. As the days grew shorter and colder, and the icy blasts swept the streets, I shivered in my thin clothes, thinking more and more of the warmth and ease of the tropics. My work, although it kept me warm during the day, only added to my discomfort. After sitting in front of glowing heater filaments all day, the icy wind was all the colder, brutally chilling my body seconds after the heavy door closed behind me. I quickly developed a vicious cough and, mindful of my bout with pneumonia, began to worry.

A smooth talking young Siamese began initiating me in the first few of the Thousand Delights of the sprawling Oriental metropolis. Many a cold night when I should have been in bed, with a hot brick at my feet, I trudged at his side along some alley in search of pleasure. It was obviously high time for a change, even I recognized this. The pleasures I could have endured -- for a time. The state of my health was a different matter. I was only twenty years old, but felt much older as the cough worsened, and every deep breath sent knives through my chest. I thought and dreamed of nothing but balmy tropical breezes perfumed with the fragrance of countless blossoms, of white beaches and swaying palms. Even heavier clothing failed to halt the chills which beset me because the cold kept pace with my ever thicker coats. My tropic-thinned blood was fighting a losing battle.

As I woke up one morning, coughing and shivering, I suddenly realized that I had to get south or die. But how? The money in my pocket would not take me three hundred miles, much less four times that far. Walking disconsolately along the crowded streets toward Soochow Creek, my head bent against the biting wind, a thought came to me, faintly at first and then stronger. I looked up. Across a small plaza, framed by evergreens, its thick dome and lofty windows dwarfing the surrounding buildings, its massive door ajar, stood a church. I had seen it often on my way to work, even pausing once to read the lettering hewn into the stone stating that it was the Anglican Church. Now I walked slowly across the square and, after a half-guilty look around, entered. No one was there. I halted before the bare altar, sank to my knees and bowed my head. I have forgotten the prayer, except that it was fumbling and halting, and fervent. I didn't know it then but it was a classic example of a foxhole prayer.

Somewhat more cheerful but still shivering, I went to work. At four o'clock I pocketed my wages, it being Friday and payday, informed the Russian foreman that I would not be back, and left. A half hour later, as I strode along the Bund, I felt a tap on my shoulder. I stopped and turned. A young, thin white man stood there. He introduced himself then mentioned seeing me at the German Consulate. This done, he lost no time coming to the business at hand. The German steamer *Donau* was in need of a messman. Would I be interested? Indeed, I would. The *Donau* was sailing for Manila that night.

As once before, on approaching the Tropic of Cancer, my health returned. Each hour, in response to the ever balmier winds, my cough became lighter, the knives in my chest less sharp until, with our arrival in Hong Kong, I could once again freely and fearlessly draw deep, life-giving breaths.

An hour before sailing a troupe of Russian chorus girls embarked and lost little time spreading consternation among the crew, walking and lounging about scantily clad and behaving in a most distracting manner, obviously not at all concerned with our peace of mind.

We arrived at Manila just before the Customs and Immigration offices closed, and two hours later I was sitting with Nenita on the window sill overlooking crowded Calle R. Hidalgo, conversing softly. I was happy to be <u>home</u> again. She insisted that her prayers to the Virgin Mary brought me back. I agreed readily. It mattered little to me who was instrumental in my return and I was therefore quite happy to give Mary the credit and so please the earnest girl beside me.

During the following days I began having serious thoughts about my status in a society of Catholics, reasoning that my chances for work or marriage would be immensely enhanced if I were one of them, instead of always having to explain my atheistic background. So I went to church, lofty, stately San Sebastian Church, bowing, genuflecting, mumbling with the others, and upon leaving, dipping my fingers in the often empty holy water vessel. When Nenita one day introduced me to her cousin Consuelo, an utterly bewitching mestiza of seventeen, I knew that the Church of Rome was about to claim another unenthusiastic convert. As I dropped off to sleep that night, listening to the soft strumming of a guitar somewhere in the house, I didn't know that I was closing one more chapter in my wandering and that, as the day dawned, I would open the final pages of my youth.

On the left, Nenita, the girl who almost caused me to become a Catholic. On the right her sister, Charito, in native costume. Both photos from the author's collection.

26

I Become Engaged

After a leisurely breakfast, I descended the polished stairs, pausing briefly before a large picture of Christ. Dutifully, for the girls were watching, I crossed myself. It was my first day at job hunting after returning from Shanghai. As it was still early, I decided to pay the Gospel Ship a visit. I calculated she should be just about ready to sail again. But the anchorage off the Manila Hotel was empty. Disappointed, I stared seaward. Had she already sailed, or had she not even arrived yet? Since it was not far to the First Baptist Church, I turned in that direction. It would only take a few minutes to drop in and ask about the ship.

    A short while later I stood in the church lobby, aware of the peculiar fragrance I associated with funeral parlors. The few young men and women who walked past me seemed preoccupied and sad, quite unlike their usual cheerful selves.

Then I saw it, the flower-draped casket in a side room. Several seminary students stood around, conversing softly and sending an occasional mournful glance at the coffin. A comely young woman, the same who was so flustered at my remark about beer during a party the previous year, stood by the coffin, her head bowed, a handkerchief clutched in one hand. Now and then a little sob escaped her, as she closed her eyes tightly.

Several students, books under their arms, halted a few steps away, nodded a greeting upon seeing me, then whispered quietly among themselves. I heard only fragments, "... released from his suffering...in heaven now...no more pain or tears... wonderful...eternal life." It was enough. Suddenly, as I glanced at the coffin, I was afraid. In an instant I relived my brushes with death: the near collision at sea, those terrible nights in the Dairen hospital, the agonizing moments on the ocean floor. What if I died at one of those times? The man who lay in the coffin, who once stood where I stood, who breathed and talked and smiled, who reveled in the sunlight, who listened to the sweet song of the birds. The man who once, too, had loved a girl, (was it she who sadly bent over him?). Had he just gone into oblivion, as my father had been so certain? Or was there, indeed, something more than was apparent, something beyond my ken? And the Bible, could it be more than a mere collection of fables and myths?

My thoughts weren't lucid or coherent as I stood there, restlessly shuffling my feet. But they were there, nevertheless, jumbled perhaps and disjointed, but very real and terribly unnerving. Oh, I knew what faith was all about, all right. Not in vain had I suffered through countless Bible classes. But I also knew my father's teachings. Unless I made a complete about-face, I would accomplish nothing. I could not hold two conflicting beliefs.

Thoroughly upset, I left the building. In the bright sunlight once again, my depression eased a little, my spirits

The Islands of the Sulu Sea

rose. Crossing the courtyard behind the seminary, I knocked on the screen door of the senior missionary's house.

Over a glass of lemonade, he told me that the yacht lay at anchor, four hundred miles to the south. Both the captain's children were sick. The engineer had quit, leaving the ship stranded. The missionary's eyes searched mine. Would I go south and bring the yacht to Manila?

I thought for a long moment, aware of a sudden, curious sensation of well-being, a feeling of joy akin to that of a man who has escaped death and walks in the warm sunlight once again. I could not see my smile, but I know it was bright.

The new year was two weeks old when I eased my thundering engine to a stop, wiped my oily hands on a hunk of cotton waste, and tumbled, fully-clad, into my bunk. Even before the ship had swung into the wind, a stone's throw from the Manila Hotel, I was asleep. It was 11 p.m. I had been awake for seemingly endless hours, anxiously watching the fuel supply as it dropped dangerously low, so low, indeed that as we entered Manila Bay, I had both fuel tanks opened and scooped out the few gallons which the pump couldn't reach with milk tins to keep the ship's great heart beating. When I finally stopped the engine, a single gallon remained in the service tank.

When I awoke the next morning, the sick children, with their mother and their *amah* or nanny, were ashore. That afternoon, Captain Skolfield took me aside and offered me the chief engineer's berth. I had no license, but neither had Mr. Davis. Licenses in those days, particularly on yachts, weren't the all-important bits of paper they are today. Without hesitation I nodded and shook his hand.

We remained in Manila for little over a month. When we sailed, on a crisp morning in February, two things had greatly changed: I had not only accepted the Baptist faith, I was also in love. In love with the comely girl who was so shocked at my remark about beer, and who bent sadly over a coffin. But for Sorsing, I might have reverted to my former indifference toward things religious. Because of her the future already looked brighter.

During that month I spent every free moment with Sorsing, dogging her steps and sometimes, I'm sure, making a nuisance of myself. Familiar with the methods of courting a girl of the East, I wooed her most slyly. So slyly in fact, that at the outset she had no idea that instead of a "brother," she actually had a suitor. She was a Baptist, and I missed no church service, no prayer meeting, never suspecting, as I listened to the sermons and sung the hymns, that my long exposure to the Baptist religion was subtly and quietly working a change that in the end would convert me to that faith.

Wooing Sorsing was not at all easy for I had three things against me from the start. I was not a Christian, I was white, and I was a sailor. The first obstacle was overcome when I became a Christian, but I could do nothing about the other two. The problem was further complicated by the utterly frustrating fact that, in accordance with local custom, I was never alone with her, and therefore unable to whisper the words of love which I longed to share with her. Notes and letters are but poor substitutes for softly murmured words. But, as always before and often since, I had reckoned without fate. One sultry afternoon, while thunderheads were piling high, promising a cooling shower, I received the word I yearned to hear. She stood on a wide porch, her arms circling a lofty pillar, looking down at me, for I stood at the foot of a short flight of stairs. Visiting hours were over and for one unexpected moment we were alone. Not very hopefully, for it had been in vain before, I again asked the timeless question. Her eyes were bright and her red lips parted, "Yes," she whispered, "yes" and fled into the house.

My heart sang as I went my way, figuratively walking on clouds or what had been clouds only a few minutes before, for it started drizzling. But now another obstacle presented itself, one that caused me no little anxiety. Soon I would have to face her parents, who lived in the south. Asking for their daughter's hand was no mean undertaking in a society in which a parent's wish is law, and where obedience a compulsion. Again, I forgot to put my trust in God. Only a little reasoning would have assured me that, having picked a girl for me half a world from home, He would certainly see the thing through. But I didn't reason, rather I fretted and stewed and worried.

27

Rites and Rituals

We cleared squat, glowering Corregidor early in the afternoon. Standing beside the hot, thundering engine, I flexed my knees in rhythm with the yacht's slow pitching as she met the China Sea swells. Life looked good indeed. My aimless wanderings were over. My doubts and questions had been answered. I had found God, and for the first time in my life a girl -- the right girl -- would be waiting for me when I returned from a voyage.

I purposely delayed my baptism so that Captain Skolfield could perform the ceremony. He was the first person to open the Bible to me, whose long and patient teaching had finally borne fruit. Also, I wanted to be baptized in the sea, under a laughing sky, in the warm water off a curving, palm-fringed beach of a far away isle. The day came a few weeks later, exactly as I envisioned it. I saw the low, lush island appear one morning, as I had seen countless others, always thrilled at the sight, even though it never varied. There is nothing quite like the sight of a tropical island rising slowly from the tranquil sea. The tips of the coconut trees are seen first, lines of dark green tufts like bouquets drifting on the ocean. Then, softly, if the breeze is just right, the scent of the isles comes across the blue water. Soon the ship is engulfed in warm perfume, the fragrance of tropical flowers, spiked with the sharp scent of spices. Sometimes, the isle whence comes the heavenly fragrance is still unseen below the horizon.

Behind us, as we stood on the beach, which swept east and west in a huge half circle, the tall supple coconut palms stood motionless, their wide fronds sharply outlined against the dark blue sky. A faint, blue-gray haze drifted through the grove, for it was almost noon, and the cooking fires were going in the village beneath the trees. Nearby, a few fishing boats lay on the sand, their masts, like thin fingers, pointing to the sky at all angles. Seaward, the yacht lay at anchor on the mirror-smooth sea, looking for all the world like a swan on a placid lake. High up, blue-white, feathery mares tails heralded high winds, but below land and sea drowsed serenely under the midday sun.

The sand was black, as it frequently is on volcanic islands. Not the inky blackness of a mourner's band, but gold with a layer of charcoal as one soon discovers on letting the dry grains trickle through one's fingers. Only when it is moistened by the lapping wavelets does the sand darken.

Many others were baptized that same day, men and women of different color and race, temperament and philosophy, yet all brothers and sisters by virtue of their common belief. In a way we were blood brothers and sisters, united by the blood of Christ and the waters of the sea. As each one emerged from the ocean, onlookers sang, "Happy day, when Jesus washed my sins away," the voices muffled by the sand. The baptismal service over, and exuberantly spurning the boat, I plunged into the clear water and swam for the ship.

Once again, weeks turned into months, but although the routine was as before, it was not monotonous. I found myself interested in the work. Also, I spent a great deal of time writing letters to Sorsing even though I never knew where I might mail them.

I still made many excursions ashore in search of diversion. It was on one of these that I came upon a funeral procession wending its way along a dusty road to the bare and dreary little cemetery just outside a village. The casket, unadorned and unpainted, was carried on the shoulders of two men, followed by a few silent men and women. A half dozen yards ahead of the coffin, four musicians played some lively tunes, which I didn't recognize. But as the pall bearers approached the grave, the still-dewy morning air rang with the zestful and cheery notes of "Happy Days Are Here Again." Since the occasion was obviously not a happy one, I could only conclude that the musicians didn't know any funeral pieces. It was just as well. It took some of the sadness away.

I climbed a low hill overlooking the sea on the opposite side of the island and saw a strange sight. About two hundred yards from the beach four boats floated on the still water while their occupants busily did their laundry in the sea. Looking closer, I noticed that each boat lay near the center of a roughly circular ring of water considerably darker than that around it. I knew at once what I was looking at, having heard about it before -- fresh water bubbling from undersea wells. Later that day, in company of a shipmate, I swam out from the rocky beach. Abruptly, as I entered the circle of fresh water, the temperature dropped sharply, sending a violent shock through my body. Dipping my head, I drank. There was only a faint trace of salt, owing perhaps to the fact that I was not in the center of the upwelling column of sweet water. It was a marvelous experience.

Near-rebellion, not to call it by the more apt name of mutiny, flared one Sunday morning in early May. A second year seminary student who, to gain experience as an evangelist, had signed on as a seaman, approached the captain and, pointing to the open Bible in his hand, informed him that since the First Day was a day of rest according to the Word, the crew would no longer wash the decks down on a Sunday morning. To my amazement, the skipper, confronted with what in sailing ship days would have set the cat-o-nine tails into action, only smiled.

"Very well," he said, nodding. "But it seems hardly fair that some should work, doing their duty, while others rest." He beckoned to me and I stepped forward. "You will not run the generator today. We won't need the lights. And you," he pointed to the cook, "will not prepare any meals. Today," his voice rose a trifle, and his smile thinned, "is a day of rest for all of us."

Consternation showed on the student's face.

"Perhaps we should not read into the Bible what is not there," cautioned the skipper.

At seven-thirty we sat down to a hearty breakfast. Below, the generator hummed softly, and outside, the clean, wet deck glistened in the morning sun.

That evening, as some of us frequently did, we rowed ashore and were soon sitting on the long bamboo bench outside the Chinese *sari-sari* store chewing away on sticky rice cakes and sipping luke-warm lemonade. The atmosphere was hot and heavy under the coconut trees, the heaviness accented by the scent of night blossoms. Every few minutes the grating call of a Tocko lizard echoed through the grove.

At the sudden sound of music we sat upright. Faintly at first, then louder it came to us through the night, the dull boom of a drum, the blare of brass. Then we saw little flickering lights dancing among the trees.

I put my half empty bottle aside and stood up just as the procession reached us. In the vanguard, with slow, measured steps, marched a band consisting of drum, two trombones, a tuba, and a trumpet. Only the drummer was active at the moment, his deep boom, boom, boom in time with his stride. Behind them, dressed in white with a rhinestone tiara in her straight, black hair, her hands clutching a crucifix, solemnly walked a little girl of perhaps five years. Her plump cheeks were thickly rouged, her small mouth daubed heavily with carmine lipstick. The rest of her face, as well as her neck, were generously coated with white talcum powder. Behind her, holding, but occasionally dropping, the train of her long, white gown, trudged two still younger girls, each flanked by a little, spruced up boy. Trailing them in ragged formation were some twenty small children, each carrying a burning candle. On both sides walked anxious adults, re-lighting candles, scolding in subdued voices, or pushing, not always gently, the moppets into place. As they passed by, the band struck up a dirge-like tune, which the youngsters picked up instantly, if a bit discordantly, until the trees rang with bright young voices. "Santa Maria, Madre de Dios..."

About twenty feet behind the children a life-size statue of the Virgin rode on a pedestal tied to a cart. Stiff and cold in her jeweled gown of white silk she wore a huge halo, from which the gold paint had peeled in spots, fastened by a wire to her neck. She carried a babe in her arms. The cart was flanked by six men carrying candles. In the flickering lights and dancing shadows she looked not at all benign, moving so stiffly, staring so fixedly, and I felt the gooseflesh form on my arms. When she was past I turned my attention to the remainder of the procession. Behind the statue walked the adult counterpart of the little girl, an extraordinarily beautiful woman of about twenty. She, too, wore a white dress of shimmering silk. In one hand she held a lighted taper while with the other she gracefully lifted the hem of her dress off the dusty road. A small crown perched a little crookedly on her shining black hair gave a jaunty, endearing look to her countenance. The candle light danced in her dark eyes; a little smile played about her red lips. She walked gravely, regally, her head held high, like the queen -- for a day -- that she was. Two almost equally comely girls carried their queen's long train. They were followed by a crowd, all bearing candles and singing the same hymn over and over. Another small band of musicians brought up the rear.

Suddenly, from the shadows appeared half a dozen weird creatures, dancing and whirling like dervishes along the entire procession. Wearing costumes of nipa leaves, they sported rooster's tails and masks in the shape of rooster heads. Dancing in and out of the shadows, illuminated by the fitful candle light, they gave the appearance of flitting demons, giving the procession a decidedly pagan look.

We could still hear the music and the singing, and see the lights winking among the trees, when we rowed back to the ship an hour later. At that moment, a thousand such processions were slowly wending their ways along paved city streets and dusty village roads from Luzon in the north to Cebu in the south and would continue, with a different "queen" but with the same idol, every night to the end of May. It was an effort to gain a few more indulgences, a few less years in Purgatory, a little more rice on the table, a little less sickness.

28

The Engine Explodes

We sailed at dawn, while a blue haze still hid the hills behind the village and countless bats fluttered silently overhead toward their caves. I set the throttle to the fourth notch from the top, a leisurely 175 r.p.m. driving the yacht along at nine knots, her most economical speed. After a short entry in the log book, I turned the engine room over to my assistant, then climbed to the bridge and watched the sun rise from its bed of fire. Taking deep breaths of the invigorating salt air, I little suspected that before the day was over I would once more teeter at the brink of eternity.

Shortly after breakfast a sea began building. By noon the wind was blowing with such force that it produced waves of alarming heights. It was a brilliant day with a cloudless sky. The wild whitecaps were blinding to look at. Ten miles ahead, and directly upwind, lay our destination, a flat, low island only partially visible above the curvature of the sea. Two hours later we were within three miles of the sheltered lee side when my assistant, who took the watch at twelve-thirty, reported a hot bearing.

I hastened to the engine room. The bearing was smoking. It would be only a matter of time before it seized the shaft, crippling the engine. If that happened the ship would immediately lose headway and be at the mercy of the huge waves. With trembling fingers I mixed a solution of flaked graphite and oil which the assistant, kneeling on the floor plates, dripped slowly into the bearing. It was my fervent hope that the graphite would flush out whatever caused the heating. Through the speaking tube I informed the captain of our predicament and requested permission to reduce speed. He agreed to half ahead, which would give the ship bare steerage way. Lowering the throttle, I returned to the bearing which, the assistant reported, seemed to be cooling. I laid my hand on the casing. The temperature had indeed gone down. As I straightened, I felt the ship nose down, and a moment later a wave overwhelmed the bridge and crashed through the skylight above the engine. As the cold water poured over the engine, the number one cylinder exploded with the crack and roar of a thunderclap. A glowing sliver of steel whirred past my temple, wedging itself into the bulkhead behind me. A solid column of fire, like a geyser of blood from a severed artery, shot from the gaping cylinder bore and fanned out against the engine room overhead. The great heart shuddered, faltered and stopped under the pressure of the propeller as the stern settled.

On the bridge, Captain Skolfield acted swiftly, well aware that it would be only minutes before the ship, bereft of power, would turn broadside to the waves and capsize. Even before ascertaining the extent of the damage from the engineers, he ordered the sails hoisted to gain some measure of control. But the flapping canvas was torn to ribbons the instant it was freed. In a desperate effort to halt the heedless swing of the ship, he ordered the port anchor dropped. A hundred fathoms below, the flukes caught hold, the chain stiffened — and parted — but not before it had yanked the bow around to face the waves once more. The yacht was momentarily safe. But the wind quickly caught her and, as if bent on suicide, she veered rapidly. The starboard anchor and the spare were dropped simultaneously. The spare hawser, a six inch manila, tightened like a bowstring and snapped with a vicious hiss, but it, too, had served its purpose, for the yacht lay once more into the wind. The remaining anchor dragged along the bottom, finding no hold, but creating enough drag to keep the bow windward. Abruptly it caught. The chain grew taut and held, the anchor a hundred twenty fathoms below the surge of the water. That was the exact length of the chain. There was no more to pay out. The island had disappeared.

Entering my cabin shortly after the explosion, I saw that the desk, with the exception of a two inch spot near the center, was covered with newspapers and magazines that had slipped from bunk and shelves. And in that small space lay a steel sliver from the cylinder head. It had burned a hole deep into the surface of the desk but hadn't touched the papers. I shuddered when I saw how close we came to having a fire at sea.

Much later, as I dug the piece of steel from the bulkhead in the engine room, I realized on what a slender thread my life hung. A mere fraction of an inch separated me from instant death. The difference this time was that I had a new faith and the belief in a life even beyond the grave. But, nevertheless, I was glad that the hot, jagged sliver missed me.

It was weeks before we collected all the splinters. Except where it was bolted down, the cylinder head had disintegrated in a cloud of red hot projectiles that filled the air of the engine room. The compressed air flasks showed numerous scratches and gouges. If one of them had gone...I dared think no further.

For three days, while the yacht tossed and pitched and rolled wildly, we climbed around the top of the engine, slipped on the oily deck, and skinned our knuckles wrestling with the heavy spare cylinder head. Twice we had it bolted down only to discover that it leaked because we were unable to tighten the big nuts sufficiently in the wild bouncing.

I don't even recall doing it, but a few days later, as I tried to reconstruct the event for entry into the log, I noted that I had made one entry concerning the accident, a laconic, "at 2:15 p.m. number one cylinder blew up."

I had neither washed nor shaved, let alone bathed for days. I was content to drop into my bunk in the littered cabin at the end of seemingly endless hours of toil, too weary even to remove my clothing. So it was with a great deal of pleasure that I took my first leisurely bath a bare hour after we dropped our single anchor in the still water just off the beach. Someone brought me a flat, hand size pumice-like stone and I spent a good half hour slowly rubbing the stone over my skin until the last vestige of grime had been dislodged, leaving the skin glowing and clear.

The use of stones as bathing implements struck me as strange when I first came across the custom, but I quickly found how wonderfully a stone cleansed and stimulated the skin. Long ago, too, I discovered other useful gifts of nature: the bark of a certain tree made a remarkable shampoo, leaving hair lustrous and soft; the oil of the coconut kept skin pliant; plain wood ashes served as soap or could be used to scour pots and pans until they shone; bamboo splinters worked as toothpicks, coconut shells made good cups and banana leaves acted as plates. There was even a leaf that resembled and was used as sandpaper. How simple life can be, yet how complicated and frenzied we manage to make it. As I matured and saw life in a vastly different perspective, as I traveled from island to island and sat at the table or on the floor with my gracious hosts, I realized increasingly how little a man requires, and how perfectly happy he can be in a land where time has been mastered and where simplicity is a way of life. A plate of steaming, fragrant rice, a fish or two fresh from the sea and broiled over a slow fire, a small piece of juicy meat, a bowl of greens, a thick slice of papaya, made a meal many a lord would envy had he but the courage to admit it.

29

The Ship Sinks

Late June found us once more on the Borneo coast. The skipper decided to bypass the Tawi-tawi islands, so we cleared at Kudat, on the extreme northern tip of Borneo just northeast of the tiny sultanate of Brunei. A day later, we headed for the Philippines again. Sailing out of the bay, I looked for the last time on Borneo; at its mangrove-tangled shore, its dark green jungles and lofty mountains. That night, as the full moon paused briefly, as if in salute, over the cradle from which it sprang, it laid a carpet of mottled gold across the gently heaving sea. I stood in the stern and gazed at the dark strip of land low on the horizon, a strange sadness in my heart...gazed until it was gone.

It had been almost two years since the yacht was dry-docked. As the barnacles grew thicker on hull and propeller, the speed went down and the fuel consumption went up. In addition, a few of the copper sheets, which covered the hull below the waterline, were torn and gouged by coral. It would be only a matter of time before the wood swarmed with marine borers. Combining a minute examination of the charts with his intimate knowledge of the area, the captain decided to beach the ship, in the manner of old time pirates and explorers. He selected a white sand cove near the village of Araceli on the island of Dumaran off the eastern coast of Palawan. It was an ideal location. The small cove was accessible by a narrow inlet and shielded from the winds by hills and tall coconut trees. There was only one drawback. The cove was infested with crocodiles, for the backwater terminated in a mangrove swamp, the favorite lair of these saurians. But as we had no intention of swimming, we decided this was no real problem.

We anchored in the center of the cove until high tide. Then, after dropping a kedge anchor far astern, the skipper pointed the bow at a spot he'd selected on the beach. He wanted the water sufficiently deep to keep the stern afloat when the tide went out, yet expose all but the aft part of the vessel's hull. At the still-higher tide the next day, with the work completed, the plan was to heave the ship off the beach with the kedge. We headed for the shore at half speed. In the engine room I felt the sharp shock of the grounding which was almost immediately followed by "Finished With Engines" on the telegraph. The ship lay at a twenty degree angle and I could hear the bilge water rushing aft. Sounding the bilges, I found the water was two inches deep.

Stepping on deck, I saw that the yacht had surged far up the beach. Her figurehead and jib boom dwarfed the few villagers who watched the maneuver and were now standing under the starboard anchor.

As the hot tropic night fell, the sailors, armed with wire brushes, scrapers, chisels and hammers, clambered over the side. In the glare of cluster lights they attacked the fouled bottom laid bare by the receding water. I slid down a rope, walked up the beach and looked at the ship. Now that the tide was down, the stern had dropped with it, increasing the angle of tilt until the vessel seemed poised to slide backward into the deep water. I climbed back on board and prepared for bed. In the village, the yellow flickering lights had long ago gone out. Only the ship was ablaze with lights, as the still air rang with the harsh sounds of scrapers, brushes, and hammers.

As was my habit before turning in, I checked the bilges. Even before dipping the stick into the oily water, I knew we were in trouble. The water had risen to within two feet of the deck plates. I lowered the stick. Six feet of water! I raced to the bridge cabin, where the captain customarily slept on hot nights. Together we hurried to the aft staterooms. A foot of water covered the cabin floors. Somewhere, the yacht had sprung a leak. It became immediately clear that unless we pumped the bilge, the ship, weighed down by the water within her, would not lift with the already rising tide which, at its height, could flood her entirely. Tersely, the skipper ordered the work on the hull stopped and the pumps started. But it soon became evident that the water was gaining the upper hand. I made a mark on a cabin wall. In a few minutes the water had risen an inch. A few sailors worked feverishly to shift the ballast, heavy rocks, from the area around the rudder post, the most likely source of the leak. When the layer of rocks was removed we saw the water bubbling from a hole near the post.

The water was waist deep in the after cabins when I volunteered to dive under the stern and try to spread a tarpaulin across the leak. Only such an emergency measure could impede the inrushing water. The skipper shook his head. The crocodiles. On my insistence he reluctantly agreed. A cluster light was hastily slung over the stern and a boat tied off close to the rudder. In it were three seamen armed with boat hooks and spears. Diving deeply, holding on to the propeller, I eased myself upward. As I looked at the black mass of ship looming over me, a water-logged settling ship, that at any moment might slide into the deep, carrying me with it, a terrible fear seized me. Frantically, my lungs aching, I groped and felt until I thought I located the leak. Surfacing, I ordered the tarpaulin slung beneath the stern. My next task would be to guide it into place. The water, meanwhile, had become alive with jelly fish, squid, and water snakes drawn by the light. It took all the agility of the men in the boat to keep the creatures at a distance.

The shape of the stern precluded a close fit of the tarpaulin, but at last it was in place, although even in the murky light I could see that it wasn't at all tight. Rising to the surface I felt a searing pain, as if a white hot poker were drawn along my right thigh from groin to foot, then another and another until my leg seemed encased in flame. I had run into a jellyfish with long tentacles, a giant Portuguese Man o' War. The shock stunned me momentarily and I felt myself sinking, but strong arms grasped me, hauling me into the boat. There I lay panting and sick, the fiery threads still sticking to my leg. A sailor lifted one tentacle, held it up and dropped it into the sea. It was longer than his reach.

I sat up and looked at my leg. Thick, red welts were forming, running all the way to my foot. Climbing aboard, I reported to the doctor. The ointment he smeared on quickly removed the sharp pain, leaving a dull ache.

The tarpaulin did little to stem the inexorable rise of the water and at 2 a.m. it reached the generator. We sloshed through the warm water, unbolted the generator and hoisted it through the skylight. The batteries were now our only source of power, and they wouldn't last long. The fuel tanks, completely submerged, were spilling through the vent pipes and a thick layer of diesel oil covered the surface of the water in the engine room, further aggravating the burns on my leg.

The Gospel Ship aground and sunk, a condition no seaman ever wants to encounter. Fortunately, after several weeks, she was refloated and continued her mission. From the author's collection.

The after staterooms were steadily filling, and as the water reached the switches the lights came on and the galley bell rang, as if controlled by spirits. The effect was weird until I shut the power off. At 3 a.m. the skipper ordered the pumping stopped. Our efforts were useless.

Ashore, the villagers slept peacefully, unaware of our plight. With the stopping of the pump, a deep silence descended on the ship, broken only by an occasional gurgling or sighing of escaping air as the water stealthily filled the compartments below. At 4 a.m. the water had risen to within two feet of the cylinder heads. My cabin, lying forward, was half full of water. The ship was settling fast, and just as the first pink rays of dawn tinted the high clouds, the sea rolled over the stern and surged forward.

In company of three men I was floundering in the oily water of the engine room in an effort to save the batteries when I felt the movement. Fearful of being trapped, I yelled to them to clear out. In the darkness we heaved ourselves toward the one still available exit. Before the first man reached the door, the ship began falling to starboard. She's capsizing, I thought, desperately fighting the sideways rushing water. One by one we lunged through the door and up the almost unclimbable stairs. The vessel stopped at an acute angle just as we got to the top. The skipper sat on the port rail, a sick look on his round face.

While I was in the water the pain of my burned skin was bearable, but the instant air struck it, it became excruciating and could be assuaged only by immersing my leg in water again. Still covered with diesel, I sat down on the slanting deck and slid into the cooling water. I stayed there all day, sliding farther down as the tide receded, and up again when it came in. The ship, a lively thing of beauty only the day before, lay like a piece of driftwood on the white beach, the incoming tide booming hollowly in her dead hull.

When the sun set, I climbed gingerly out of the water and stood up. My leg still burned, but now only like a bad sunburn. The agonizing pain was gone. I filled a bucket with water from the port deck tank, washed the oil from my skin, and put on clean clothes. Fortunately I had thrown a few things into a suitcase before my cabin flooded.

The skipper rented a few huts. A bright fire was going in the makeshift galley when I reached it and the fragrance of rice and roasted fish was very inviting indeed, especially as I had had nothing to eat since the previous evening.

Luckily, the ship's storeroom was located on the port side, forward and had, in consequence, escaped the flooding, as had the crew's quarters. Thus, well supplied with food we began a two-month sojourn in an idyllic little village on a small island in the Sulu Sea. Two days later, the skipper left on a coast guard cutter. In response to our call it had turned aside from its regular course. The mail steamer was not due for another month. The skipper grinned when he said goodbye. It was, he said, time for his vacation anyhow. Meanwhile he would try to get a salvage ship to us. I gave him a package of letters to Sorsing in which I explained why I could not visit her as planned.

The handful of Christians in the village had built a small church, and there, one quiet Sunday morning, I took a deep breath and preached my first, and last, sermon -- on the subject of Faith. After our problems with the ship I felt well qualified.

A full month after the mishap a salvage crew arrived. The yacht was made watertight (we thought) and presently the pump was discharging a steady stream of water into the bay. When, after several hours, the water level in the ship stayed the same, a diver discovered a broken ten inch porthole in the captain's stateroom. A patch was quickly fabricated to cover it. No longer required to pump the bay dry,

Capt. Hastings of the salvage crew and the hut that served as his toolshed. We slept in similar huts while the ship was refloated. From the author's collection.

the big pump made short work of the water and as the sun went down on the second day, the yacht lay once more at anchor, bedraggled and dirty, a few yards from the beach.

Then followed weeks of unceasing toil, of washing, scraping, drying out, painting. We took the engine apart piece by piece, racing against the rust, which began its attack the moment the air touched the metal. From dawn to dusk we washed and oiled like men possessed, and covered every inch of the engine room deck with parts. Only when night came, serene and lovely, did we rest, grateful for the silence, the balmy air, the fragrance, as we walked slowly among the palms or chatted with the villagers sitting on the bench outside the single store.

It took the carpenter less than a day to find the cause of the sinking. The entire stern, from rudder up, had been eaten away by termites and was literally held together only by the paint. The insects had doubtlessly come aboard with the firewood, of which we used a great deal in the galley stove.

The skipper, looking fresh and fit, arrived on the coastal steamer and immediately decided to run the ship to Cuyo. The repair facilities were better there and a large mission house was being constructed, both requiring his supervision. As we headed for the inlet and open sea, I looked back through the porthole at the beach. It lay, undisturbed again, dazzling and clean in the morning sun.

30

The Voyage Ends

The long delay at Cuyo, while the termite-eaten timbers were replaced with iron wood, afforded me the chance to visit my — I hoped — future in-laws, to ask for their daughter's hand. She had "worked on them" and they agreed, not too happily but graciously enough. On a sparkling day in October, with a perfumed breeze ruffling the lacy curtains, I kissed Sorsing, my wife, for the first time.

For yet another half year, my wife at my side, I sailed the Sulu Sea and the China Sea on the Gospel Ship, watching men and women embrace Christianity in ever-increasing numbers; little bamboo and wood churches springing up like mushrooms. Then, one sultry evening in May, while the early monsoon clouds piled up in the southwest, I listened, with a heavy heart, as the anchor chain roared through the hawsepipe, off the Manila Hotel. Slowly, for it would be for the last time, I set the telegraph to "Finished With Engines" then let my fingers slowly trail, in a final caress, from the shiny handle. They were over, my carefree days. Henceforth I would only dream, as the poet said, of all the golden hours spent in ships, to trace, in retrospect, the days, the starlit nights....

Having thus reached the end of another, but the most important chapter in my life, I took my wife's hand and gently led her down the gangway. My long voyage was over.

The Islands of the Sulu Sea

About The Ship

Designed and built in 1913, the *Fukuin Maru* was the creation of Mr. Allan of the Allan Steamship Line of Glasgow. He gave the vessel to the American Baptist Foreign Mission Society in memory of his mother with the intent that it be used in the evangelization of the islands and coastline of the Inland Sea of Japan. It measured 120 feet long with a beam of 24 feet and was made of wood with copper sheeting covering the entire hull. It had two masts, two mainsails and two jibs. Main propulsion was provided by an oil burning Bolinder engine, made in Stockholm, Sweden which produced a speed of nine knots. There was an auxiliary engine connected to a dynamo which provided electricity. Accommodations included a galley with two stoves, three cabins for passengers — each with two berths, four one-berth cabins, and a six-berth cabin for crew members. Fuel capacity was 800 gallons. There was a medical dispensary on board measuring six foot square. Lifesaving apparatus consisted of two lifeboats and a small tender. Her first master was Captain Luke Bickel, who sailed the Inland Sea of Japan doing missionary work for ten years. He was succeded by Captain James Laughton, who continued the ministry for another five-and-a-half years. In 1928 it was decided that the money spent in operating the *Fukuin Maru* could be put to better use elsewhere and she was sold to a Japanese ship brokerage in Kobe, Japan. The brokers intended selling the vessel into the fishing trade, but couldn't find a buyer. The vessel sat in Kobe harbor for three years carrying an asking price of $14,000.

Meanwhile, the Baptist mission in the Philippines, which for several years wanted a ship for its work, received a bequest of $10,000 -- provided it be used to purchase the *Fukuin Maru*.

Capt. Skolfield, working at the mission in Manila, was dispatched to Kobe to buy the ship. He offered $7,000, the buyers dropped the price to $13,000. The captain went up to $8,000. The buyers came down to $12,000. Skolfield raised his offer to $9,000. The brokers dropped to $11,000. Finally both parties agreed on $10,000 and the deal was closed.

With another grant of $5,000 Capt. Skolfield was able to drydock the ship and get a crew and provisions for the trip to Manila. They almost didn't make it. Hitting a storm off the northern Philippines, the sails were torn to shreds. The ship was blown ever closer to shoals and reefs until the captain rigged a sea anchor using the torn sails and held the ship in deep water until the storm subsided. He arrived safely in Manila two days later. Kurt Rose joined the ship several months later.

After Kurt left the ship, it fell on difficult times. The effects of the Great Depression were felt in the Philippines on a delayed basis. By 1936 the ship was barely able to operate and then only at reduced speed to conserve fuel. For a time the *Fukuin Maru* was used as a base for mining engineers at newly discovered manganese deposits on Palawan. When the leaders of the mission learned the ship was referred to as "The Manganese Ship" and that the engineers were drinking, smoking and playing cards on board, they realized their main purpose — evangelism — was being ignored. It was time to re-establish the vessel's purpose. It was sent on a survey cruise through the Dutch East Indies and New Guinea in the fall and winter of 1938 and 1939. Then it was back to the old haunts of the Sulu Sea, the islands between Mindanao and Borneo.

When Capt. Skolfield's furlough was due in 1939, the ship was anchored in the harbor of Recordo on the island of Mindanao. With the threat of war ever closer, the captain was recruited by the United States Navy. He accepted.

The Islands of the Sulu Sea

Meanwhile, the *Fukuin Maru* sat in Recordo with a lone Philippine crewman as a watchman. She was almost thirty years old, her engines were worn out, white ants were eating at the hull planking. She badly needed drydocking and repairs but the cost was prohibitive. For a while, the idea of scuttling the ship in the open sea, "a Christian burial," was considered. The ship was offered to the Navy for use in the coming war and, after some hesitation, accepted. The ship was being towed to Manila for repairs on December 8, 1941 when the bases at Pearl Harbor, Hawaii and Subic Bay and Cavite in the Philippines were hit. The ship was never heard from again.

Or was she? Conjecture was that our own Navy may have scuttled her rather than let her fall into the hands of the Japanese. However, Rev. Henry DeVries, Sr., who was captured and interned by the Japanese in Mindanao, was sure he saw the vessel in the harbor at Davao, Mindanao during the Japanese occupation. He said he could not mistake the trim-lined, two masted schooner. If so, then it was probably sunk during the American liberation of the Philippine Islands in 1944 and 1945.

The Islands of the Sulu Sea

About The Author

Kurt Rose was born in 1914 in Dresden, Germany, the son of a gentle Saxon mother, who died when he was very young, and a stern Prussian father. At the age of fifteen, he ran away to sea. After the adventures chronicled in this book, he settled in Manila, working for the Luzon Stevedoring Company (Lusteveco), one of the largest stevedoring companies in the Far East. When the Japanese attacked, then invaded the Philippines on December 8, 1941, he found himself in a unique situation. As a German citizen, he and his family were technically allies of the Japanese. But his beliefs and his allegiance were elsewhere and he decided to wage his own war against the Axis powers. Refusing to work under the new Japanese authority at Lusteveco, he went out into Manila Bay on the last night he had access to the harbor and sabotaged the company's tugboat fleet, temporarily frustrating Japanese plans for control of Manila Bay and the seige of Corrigedor.

Throughout the war he covertly operated a homemade radio receiver and, at the risk of his own life, passed on information to Americans interned in prison camps including the infamous Santo Tomas prison camp, helping sustain their morale.

After the war, Kurt Rose returned to Lusteveco. In the 1950's he came to the United States with his wife and children. There he joined Westinghouse Corp., becoming engineer in charge of instrumentation for the Trident and Polaris missile programs.

Kurt is now retired and lives in California. He and his wife have made many return trips to the Far East, and to some of the islands of the Sulu Sea.

The Islands of the Sulu Sea

Glossary

Aft. The back end or toward the back end of a ship. Also "after" as in the after house, to differentiate it from the midships house.

Barong. 1. An open craft used for fishing in the coastal waters of Western Borneo. It is rowed or sailed. If sailed, one mast is used and carries a square sail. Steering is accomplished with twin rudders or a long oar. 2. A large, broad-bladed knife or cleaver used by the Moros. 3. A dress shirt worn by Philippine men and made of very fine pineapple fibers.

Barrio. A regional division as a section of a town or rural area.

Batil. Also called Batelao. A small coaster of the Persian Gulf and West Coast of India. Larger types have two masts while the smaller carry one. Sails are of the settee type. The vessel ranges in size from 30 to 100 tons.

Bitts. A pair of wooden or steel posts permanently attached to a vessel for fastening lines, ropes or cables.

Black Gang. The unlicensed engine crew of a steam or motor ship. The term derives from their faces being covered with coal dust (hence, black) after stoking the ship's furnaces while on watch.

Bolo. A large, single-edged knife or machete.

Bumboat. A small open boat used to carry supplies for sale to vessels in a harbor.

Carabao. A domestic water buffalo as found in the Philippines.

Copra. Dried coconut meat from which oil is extracted.

Datu. Title of the husband of a titled Moro woman, as a consort.

Davit. A small arm or derrick used aboard ship to hoist boats, anchors, ladders, stores, etc.
Durian. A large fruit of Southeast Asia having a hard, prickly skin, flavorful, pulpy flesh and an offensive odor.
Godown. A slang term used in the Far East for warehouse or storehouse, from the Malay *godong*.
Hadjii (also spelled hadji or hajji). A person of the Muslim faith who has made the pilgrimage to Mecca.
Haradryads. A poisonous snake native to Southeast Asia.
Hawsepipe. The metal pipe on a ship through which the anchor chain runs, leading from the forward deck to the outside of the hull.
Houri. One of the beautiful virgins provided in Paradise for all faithful Muslims.
Imam. The officiating priest of a Muslim mosque.
Jib, jibboom. A jib is a triangular sail carried on a stay between the tip of the bowsprit and the top of the foremast. A jibboom is a boom that serves as an extension of the bowsprit and has the purpose of supporting the stay that carries the jib.
Junk. A Chinese sailing vessel of the lugger type with a high poop and an overhanging bow.
Kampong. A native village.
Kedge. A light anchor used to "kedge" a ship from one place to another. The kedge anchor is carried out away from the ship and dropped. The ship is then pulled into position over the anchor by the anchor windlass or with a winch. Often used to pull a ship off a beach.
Kris. A short sword or heavy dagger with a wavy blade used by the Malays. Also creese or crease.
Kumpit. A small sailing vessel used for hauling cargo.
Lantaka. A small native craft of the Philippines.
Lee. The downwind (and usually sheltered) area, as the lee side of a ship or a cove in the lee of the wind.
Mah-jongg. A Chinese game played by four persons with 144

tiles and dice.
Manila. Before synthetics, all line (ropes) aboard ship was made of manila fiber and referred to as "manila line." The fibers are technically those of the Abaca, a plant native to the Philippines. Because manila line is especially stiff, resistant to moisture and unaffected by salt water, it was ideally suited to being made into "hawsers," the heavy lines used to hold a ship alongside a pier.
Mestiza. A person of mixed Philippine and Caucasian blood.
Nipa. A type of palm whose leaves are used for thatching and basketry.
Plimsoll Marks. The lines on the side of a ship which indicate the maximum depth to which it can be safely loaded. Invented by Samuel Plimsoll.
Sari-sari. A type of small store specializing in a variety of goods.
Scimitar. A curved, single-edged sword.
Tagbanua. A tribe of the island of Palawan.
Taffrail. The upper railing on the after main deck of a ship that encompasses the stern.
Tienda. A general store.
'Tween Decks. Shortened form of "between decks," meaning those decks that are between the main deck and the bottom of a ship.
Tuba. Fermented coconut milk.
Vinta. A paddling and sailing canoe of the southern Philippine Islands. It features double-outriggers and is used for fishing and transportation. Very fast under sail and wonderfully seaworthy for their size they commonly make trips of four and five days. Because of their speed they are favored by the smugglers of the Sulu Islands and Borneo.
Winch. A machine on board ship used for hoisting and hauling. Winches are hand- or power-driven and have one or more drums or barrels on which to wind chain or rope.

Index

A

Age of Discovery 70
Algeria 14
Ali Baba 19
Alliance missionaries 148
Amon 19
amuck 114
Amy 147, 150, 166, 167
Anglican Church 176
Araceli 196
Asiatic Fleet, U.S. 59
Australia 25
Avenida Rizal 33
Avenida Taft 34

B

Bab el Mandeb, Strait of 23
Bacuit 68
Bajao 165
Bajao Sea Gypsies 163
Balabac Island 95
Balabac Light 95
Balabac Strait 95
Balhalla 163
Baptist 116
Baptist Church 66, 174
Baptist Dormitory 127
Baptist Mission 63
barong 138

Bataan Peninsula 59
Batanes 90
batil 100
Battle of Manila Bay 110
Bay of Biscay 9
Bay of Mamburao 134
Beri-beri 155
Bilatoan 118
Bongao 112, 113, 147, 168
Bongao Light 110
Bontoc 86
Borneo 30, 31, 63, 98, 99, 100, 101, 106, 109, 110, 158, 163, 169, 195
Brunei 195
Bubbling Well Road 175
Buksuk 93
Bund, The 39, 175, 177
Burma 101
Busuanga Island 62

C

Cagayah Sulu 158
Cagayancillo 121
Calle R. Hidalgo 177
Canton 86, 126
Cape Melville Light 95
Cape Ross 70
Cape Sao Vicente 9
Cardiff 3

Caro, Juan and Carmen   55, 56, 61, 128
Caro, Vilma   58
Cebu   189
Celebes   109, 110, 164, 169
Celebes Sea   156
Ceylon (Sri Lanka)   25
Charybdis Shoal   79
Chimulpo   39
China   36
China Coast   125
China Sea   70, 184, 203
Chinampo   39
Chinese Pier   118, 148
Christian Missionary Alliance   119
Chungking   126
Cleopatra   19
Colombo   25
Consuelo   178
copra   141
Coron Island   65, 67
Corregidor   62, 184
Crocodile Sound   74. *See also* Malampaya Sound.
Culion   67, 135. *See* leper colony
Cuyo   77, 138, 147, 171, 173, 202, 203
Cuyo Islands   76
Cuyo passage   76

D

Dairen   47, 48, 49, 51, 52, 53, 180
Datu Ombra   150
Datubato   146
Davis, Mr.   126, 135, 148, 149, 181
Dayang-dayang   148, 150
Denmark   6
Dewey Boulevard   130
Donau   177

Driftwood Point   96
Duisburg   52, 175
Dumaran   196
Dyak   103, 107

E

Egypt   16
Elbe   6, 34
Emergency Point   70
English Channel   9
Enterprise Point   70
Equator   26
Escolta   33
Eta Rickmers   3, 9

F

Fairy Queen   70
Farjoe, Mr.   86, 125, 175
First Baptist church   179
Fragrant Harbor   36. *See* Hong Kong
French Concession   39
Fu Man Chu   37
Fukuin Maru   photo 60, 61

G

Germany   33, 78
Gethsemane   81
Gibraltar   9, 12
godown   37
Good Tidings   129. *See also Fukuin Maru*
Gospel Ship   photo 60
Great Danger Bank   95
Gulbranson, Rev. Mr.   119, 148

H

Hadjii   170, 171
Hainan   126
Hamburg   3

Harbin   47, 48
Hong Kong   7, 26, 27, 35, 36, 37, 53, 86, 103, 177
houris   115

I

Imam   153
India   78, 101
Indian Ocean   23
Indo China   70
Isis   19

J

Jahara   150
Jansen, Rev. Mr. and Mrs.   67, 135
Japan   39
Java   109, 164, 168
Jikiri the pirate   113
Jolo   118, 148
Jones Bridge   34
juramentado   114, 115

K

kampong   146
Keen, R. Caisson   106
Kobe   26, 39
Kobenhavn   3
Korea   39
kris   114
Kudat   195
Kyoto   42

L

Landis, Mr.   148
lantaka   146
Lazarus   73
Legaspi Landing Cabaret   59
leper colony   67
Leverkusen   53
liana   88

Lidvaard   3
Lord Auckland Shoal   70
Luneta   130
Luzon   61, 86, 91

M

Magellanic Cloud   145
Maimunah   118, 147, 148, 149, 150, 151, 154, 171, 172
Malampaya Sound   71, 74
malaria   155, 161
Malaya   91
Mallaca, Strait of   26
Manchuria   47
Mandarin   50
Mangaree Great Reef   96
Manila   26, 27, 30, 31, 32, 33, 36, 40, 54, 57, 82, 84, 92, 110, 111, 130, 147, 174, 177, 181
Manila Bay   31, 62, 124, 181
Manila Hotel   59, 124, 179, 203
Mantabuan   118
Marchesa Bank   96
Martha W.   6
Marudu   105, 106
Mediterranean Sea   11, 12 15
merienda   57
Middle Shoal   70
Milky Way   145
Mindanao   119
Mindoro   130, 134
Minna Reefs   96
Moji   40
Monmouth Shoals   96
Monsoon   134
Moros   109, 113, 160
Mukden   48, 51

N

Nagasaki 40, 53
Nagoya 40
Nenita 174, 177, 178
Nibelungen 81
Nordstrom 61
Nordwind 3
North Balabac Strait 93
North Borneo 102, 161
North Borneo Trading Company 102
North Sea 6, 7, 11
Nymphe Rock 96

O

Oran 14
Orangutan 99

P

Palawan 62, 68, 70, 79, 92, 93, 111, 136, 140, 173, 196
Panducan 146
Pangaturang 146
Paracale 86
Pasig River 34
Persia 78
Philippines 30, 98, 101, 119, 158, 173, 195
Pier Seven, Manila 175
Plaza Santa Cruz 33
Port Said 15, 16, 26
Portugal 9
Portuguese Man o' War 198

Q

quarantine flag 32
Queen of the Sea Shoal 79
quinine 161

R

Ra 19
Rapture 116
Rawalpindi 11
Roman Church 68, 69, 76, 121, 128, 139, 174
Royalist Rock 96
Russia 43, 46

S

Sakhalin 46
Salt pork 5
San Sebastian Church 57, 177
Sandakan 100, 162
Sanga-Sanga 118
sari-sari 188
Savoy theater 33
Scheherazade 19
Schuck, William 112, 118, 173
Sea of Japan 42
Seahorse Shoal 70
Seaman's Book 6
Seaman's Club, Vladivostok 43
Seine 34
Shanghai 13, 26, 38, 39, 48, 49, 53, 125, 126, 175, 179
Shanghai Power Company 175
Shimonoseki 40
Siam 78
Siasi 118
Siberia 42, 44, 175
Sibutu 165
Sibutu Passage 110, 165
Sikh 37
Simunul 110, 165
Singapore 26, 30
Sitankai 109, 158, 163, 165
Skolfield, David 133
Skolfield, Ellis 133
Skolfield, Capt. 61, 62, 92, 111,

121, 143, 149, 156, 169, 181, 184, 191
Skolfield, Mrs.   129, 130, 147
Soochow Creek   39, 175
Sorsing   182, 201, 203
South China Sea   30, 134
South Ubian   168, 170
Southern Cross   145
Spanish Fly   15
Strait of Gibraltar   11
Suez   21
Sultan Kiram of Sulu   149
Sultana Shoal   79
Sulu   90, 115
Sulu Archipelago   146
Sulu Islands   114, 173
Sulu Sea   31, 78, 79, 92, 113, 121, 150, 156, 163, 166, 172, 200, 203
Sumatra   26

T

taffrail   35
Tagalog   54
Tagbanua   83, 84
Tandubas   118
Tarhata   150
Tashinkiao   48
Tawi-tawi   109, 119, 165, 158, 168, 170, 172, 173, 195
Temple Bank   70
Thames   34
Thor   81
"three-islander."   3
tienda   90, 91
Tientsin   126
Tocko   188
Trans-Siberian Railroad   47
Tricolor   3
Tropic of Cancer   53, 177
Tsing-wan-tao   39

tuan   112
Tubalubac   146
Tubbataha Reef   79
Tubindangan   165
Turkey   78
typhoon   130, 131, 132

U

University of Illinois   149

V

Verde Island Passage   131, 134
vinta   100
Vladivostok   26, 42, 43, 47

W

Walkuries   81
Wallace   111
Walled City   33, 34
Wanderer Shoal   96
waterspouts   24
Wedge Island   70
windjammer   25
Woosung   38
Wotan   81

Y

Yalan Tiga   102, 103, 104, 105
Yangtze   86, 126
Yangtze Kiang   38
Yingkow   48, 49, 126
Yokohama   7, 40, 53
Yokohama Seaman's Mission   40
York Breakers   70
Yuan You   126

Z

Zamboanga   119, 120, 164